Rescue Me

The incredible true story of
the abandoned mastiff who
became a movie star

Julie Tottman

sphere

SPHERE

First published in Great Britain in 2021 by Sphere

1 3 5 7 9 10 8 6 4 2

Copyright © Julie Tottman, 2021
Text by Emily Fairbairn

A CIP catalogue record for this book
is available from the British Library.

ISBN 978-0-7515-8011-2

Typeset in Goudy by M Rules
Printed and bound in Great Britain by
Clays Ltd, Elcograf S.p.A.

Papers used by Sphere are from well-managed forests
and other responsible sources.

Sphere
An imprint of
Little, Brown Book Group
Carmelite House
50 Victoria Embankment
London EC4Y 0DZ

An Hachette UK Company
www.hachette.co.uk

www.littlebrown.co.uk

Contents

Chain Reaction

Even with the heavy chain around my neck and the evening chill seeping into my aching bones, I could still picture the tree covered in tinsel and lights. It was the first thing I had seen as I emerged from the cardboard box many months ago. Reaching back to that happy memory, I could hear the excited squeals of the humans as I tentatively stepped forward on my little paws. And, of course, I could still see Toby's delighted face swimming into view, and feel the warmth

1

and contentment that washed over me as he held me in his arms.

What I couldn't remember quite as well was where it all went wrong. They had loved me, hadn't they? Not just Toby, who was twelve, but his mum Josie and dad Martin too. Toby and I would play such crazy games, chasing each other round and round the house and rolling around on the floor, before snuggling down to snooze together. Josie would take me for walks through the town and feed me big bowls of delicious dog food. Martin – well, with Martin, it was always more complicated. He would pull my tail or flick my nose until I barked with pain. But then he'd smile at me and say, 'That's the sound of a proper guard dog.'

Maybe things started to change because I couldn't stop growing. I wished I could go back to being so small I could sit on Toby's lap but instead I just got bigger and bigger. My robust legs were like branches of a great oak tree. My paws were like saucers. Even my skin couldn't stop expanding until it hung in heavy folds all around the hefty trunk of my body.

'You stupid dog!' Josie would scream as my tail, as thick and heavy as a rope, accidentally whipped another mug of tea off the coffee table. Then she'd raise a rolled-up newspaper and whack me sharply across the face. It stung – and not just because of the physical pain. I hadn't meant to upset her – I only wanted to please. But my ever-enlarging body was getting harder and harder to control.

Even Toby seemed to have become tired of me. The moment he walked through the door after school had always been the highlight of my day. At first, it seemed like it was his highlight too, and he'd make such a fuss of me. But as the months went on, I noticed how he stopped smiling as I bounced around in excitement to greet him. 'Urghhh, MUM!!!' he would yell to Josie. 'The dog is drooling everywhere again – it's disgusting!'

My walks with Josie were getting less frequent, and the family started to leave me for ever longer periods on my own. I felt like a coiled spring, humming with energy that I didn't know what to do with.

Then, one day, I got so bored I started to chew the leg of the sofa. I never meant any harm – but it looked so tempting, and I had nothing else to do. I thought I would just nibble a bit, but once I started I couldn't stop. I gnawed away until it was a mangled stump. The sofa lurched forwards – I had chewed the leg so much that it was no longer evenly balanced – and a cushion rolled onto the floor, landing at my feet. I pricked my ears. Before I even knew what I was doing, I was ripping into the cushion, and clouds of white feathers were pluming into the air. I held the cushion in my powerful jaws and shook – how fun it was to see the whole room covered in a blanket of fluffy snow!

It was then that I heard the door open – and

the shouting began. Martin grabbed me by the collar and walloped me across the face. 'Bad dog!' he growled, and dragged me to the back door, throwing me out into the yard.

Whimpering with pain and anguish, I pressed myself against the door, desperate to be let back in so I could show them how sorry I was.

'That's it!' Josie was shouting. 'Why on earth you ever thought a Neapolitan mastiff would be a good pet is beyond me.'

'He was never meant to be a pet – he was meant to be a guard dog!' Martin roared back. 'It was you and Toby who made him soft by keeping him in the house. That dog belongs outside.'

I never set foot in the house again. I remember that first night outside in the small concrete yard, as darkness fell, and how scared and lonely I felt. I whined and whimpered in desperation, until I realised that they intended to leave me out there all night. Then I started to bark; big, deep, imploring cries for help which went unanswered, until I was so exhausted I fell into a restless sleep.

The next morning, Martin appeared. I wagged my tail happily – maybe all was forgiven? Surely they still loved me as much as I loved them?

But he hadn't come to pet me, or walk me, or even to let me back in the house. He had come to chain me up. He looped the string of heavy metal links around my neck, yanking it so roughly that I cried out in shock. Then he fastened it to the fence, and was gone.

I tried to dart after him, only to feel the heavy restraint choke me as I pulled. Then I started to bark again. I don't know how many hours I kept it up, but it fell on deaf ears.

The days all started to slip into one after that. The yard became dirty and smelly, which I knew was my fault. I had a makeshift kennel, which was really just a stack of old building materials precariously leaning against each other, with a towel laid inside. The towel was so soiled and damp that it made me shiver when I took refuge there. But when the wind howled and rain came sheeting down, what choice did I have?

When they remembered, Josie or Martin would come outside with a few scraps in a grubby bowl. Those were the good days – but they were few and far between, and my stomach always growled with a never-satisfied hunger.

Summer was long gone, and the family hardly came out into the yard any more. The best days were when Toby would slink outside, his face full of guilt and apology. My heart would burst to see my old friend, and I strained towards him, desperate for his kind touch. He would stroke my ears and give me a treat, but he never stayed long. I could see he was chilly, and I tried to lick his hands to warm him up, but he would push me away. 'I'm sorry, boy,' was all he would say as he retreated back into the warmth of the house.

The days grew ever shorter and I feared that winter might never end. It scared me how feeble I had become, and I had to use all my strength just to try to stay warm. My body felt hollow and I knew if spring didn't come soon, I wouldn't survive.

All I could do was cower in my filthy kennel, hoping for a miracle.

Then one morning, just as spring seemed on the brink of returning, I was abruptly awoken by the sharp jab of a boot making contact with my aching belly. It was Martin, who was crouching in the entrance of the kennel.

'The neighbours are sick of your barking,' he said. 'It's time to get rid of you.'

I realised he had the end of the chain in his hand, and all of a sudden he was heaving me to my feet and out of my prison. I felt a jolt of fear, but also a small spark of hope. Surely wherever I was going next couldn't be any worse than this?

Chapter One

Throw in the Owl

'And action!' I called. My team of five animal trainers, each with an owl on their shoulder, lifted their arms in unison. The hope was that the owls would start to fly in perfect circles, as we had been practising. In reality, only one of the owls did. Another swooped away, back towards the aviary where it knew dinner would later be served. Two stayed stubbornly on their trainers' shoulders. Another flapped hopefully towards me, then landed on the grass by my feet and lazily ruffled his feathers. We were in for a long six weeks getting these bird-brains ready.

It was the spring of 2004, about a month and a half away from the start of filming on *Harry Potter and the Goblet of Fire*. As head animal trainer, I was working with my team to prepare all the furry and feathered cast members for their parts in the magical movie.

We had the script and were beginning our initial groundwork, going through fundamental training with some of the animals at our base at Leavesden Studios, the HQ for the *Harry Potter* films. There were also regular meetings with the director, Mike Newell, to discuss exactly how scenes would be shot and what the animals we provided would need to do.

As *Harry Potter* was such a massive production – taking nearly a year to film each instalment, not just at Leavesden but at locations across the country – a lot of our casting and training would continue once filming had begun.

I had already lost count of the number of animals we had trained since I started working on *Potter* back in 2000, but I reckoned it was at least 150.

Right now we had twelve owls, but they would eventually be joined by nearly seventy more. One of the most ambitious scenes called for eighty owls to 'act' in the Hogwarts Owlery, while Harry Potter, played by Daniel Radcliffe, asks Cho Chang, played by Katie Leung, to attend the Yule Ball with him. While the teen actors had to capture the awkward moments of first love, it was down to the animal team to make sure all the owls were hooting, flying or sitting still at the same time. Judging by our slow progress today, it would be no mean feat if we pulled it off. Owls, if I'm honest, are particularly stupid. Ravens, which we also trained for the *Harry Potter* movies, could learn in a week what it took an owl a month to learn. But this was my fourth *Potter* now, and I had got used to the birds' idiosyncrasies. Despite the challenges we had training them, it was the owls which got the most fan mail of all the animal actors, especially Gizmo, the snowy owl who played Harry's pet Hedwig. We always tried to write back to fans with a feather enclosed with the letter.

'OK – not quite what we're looking for!' I called to the team, laughing. 'Let's take a break.'

I set off towards the Portakabin that served as our kitchen to put the kettle on, while the owl handlers – along with their stubborn charges – headed for the bird mews, a large meshed area where the birds could fly around between training sessions.

The training ground was to be our second home for the next year while we prepared for and then filmed *The Goblet of Fire*. It was essentially a couple of fields, but there was also accommodation for the animals, exercise runs for the dogs, a barn that we used as an indoor training area when it was raining and another cabin, which served as a little office. Most importantly, it was five minutes' walk from the main film studios, so once filming started we could be summoned at a moment's notice by the director.

'Those bloody owls, eh?' a familiar voice said behind me, as I dropped teabags into mugs. It was Jo Vaughan, my second-in-command and best friend. Her blond hair was pulled back in a tight ponytail, and as usual there was a hint of a smile playing around her mouth and in her bright blue eyes. Jo could always see the funny side, even when things went wrong, which was just as well – having a sense of humour is pretty essential when you work with animals. During my fourteen years as a movie trainer I had endured animals going to the toilet on expensive bits of equipment, humping A-listers' legs, going on strike just when the light was fading and the crew was most stressed – you name it, I'd faced it. On the last *Harry Potter* one of my owls had gone swooping off with the director's notes. But I had also seen animals I trained act their socks off, pulling off amazing feats which have left Hollywood stars and Oscar-winning directors speechless. When it comes to animal training, you have to take the rough with the smooth.

Jo and I had been working together since we met on the set of *102 Dalmatians* back in 1999. I was chief puppy trainer and she was the rookie on my team; it was her first film, having quit her job training sea lions at a safari park to try her luck in the movies. It had been a bit of a baptism of fire, with hundreds of puppies misbehaving and peeing all over the place, but Jo rose to the challenge masterfully.

I smiled. 'We'll get there, we always do. Even if I do wish J. K. Rowling had decided to make literally any other bird the star of the show . . .'

'Well, it's good we're scheduled to do some practice with the cats tomorrow,' said Jo, taking her mug of tea. 'I definitely need a break from owls!'

Trainers Anna, Simon, Dave and Guillaume trooped into the kitchen, noisily debating whose owl was the bottom of the class. 'It's definitely Leo,' Guillaume, an energetic Frenchman who specialised in bird training, was saying. 'But he's the best looking, so I guess he makes up for it.'

That kicked off a whole new debate about which owl was the most beautiful – the trainers could argue for hours about this kind of thing, all passionately fighting the corner of whichever bird they were in charge of. I smiled and leaned back in my chair, content to listen to them argue it out.

Harry Potter was like that – a totally immersive job where you found yourself deeply invested in whether one barn owl had a prettier face than another almost identical one.

It is mad to think now, but when I was asked to come on board the first film, *The Philosopher's Stone*, I had never even heard of the *Harry Potter* books. I remember telling friends that I had been contracted to 'some wizard film'. Little did I know that wizard film would become one of the biggest movie franchises the world had ever seen and provide me with employment for over a decade.

I always loved coming to Leavesden, not least because it meant working with a big team of talented trainers. On films that require fewer animals it was often just me on my own, or if I was lucky, Jo too. But *Harry Potter* was no ordinary film, and with a vast coterie of animal actors, I was proud to say I led one of the key departments.

I was jolted from my thoughts by the sound of the phone ringing in the office. 'OK, OK, I think the only thing we *can* agree on is they are all very silly birds,' I said, getting up from my chair. 'Can you crack on with another fifteen-minute training session with the owls, and I'll catch you up? Just got to take this.'

Shutting the door to my little office, I picked up the phone. 'Hello, Julie Tottman speaking.'

'Hi Julie, it's Pat.'

'Ah, hi Pat, so lovely to hear from you!' I said, and meant it. Pat owned Hugo, the Neapolitan mastiff who played the character Hagrid's dog Fang. Whenever there was a new *Harry Potter* film, Pat would lease Hugo to me so I could train him and bring him to the film set. He was due to start training in a couple of weeks, and ringing Pat to discuss it had been on my to-do list. 'How's your gorgeous boy? We can't wait to see him.'

'Well, about that,' said Pat, and I could hear the hesitation in her voice. 'I've got some bad news . . .'

And, just like that, the misbehaving owls were driven totally out of my mind – we had a new crisis on our hands.

Chapter Two

A Hugo Loss

Jo came to find me about twenty minutes later. 'Julie, what's happened to you?' she called as she came clattering into the office. 'You missed Leo actually doing what he was told for once!'

Then she saw my face and stopped. 'Oh God, what's happened?'

I sighed and rubbed my temples. 'That was Pat on the phone. She's worried about Hugo, who seems to have slowed down, so I've suggested she retire him.'

I should have seen it coming, I suppose. Neapolitan mastiffs are big dogs so tend to have shorter lifespans than some breeds, with most only living to about eight or nine years old. Hugo was seven, and Pat had recently noticed that he was starting to get some stiffness in his legs when she took him for a walk. It was a sign he was getting old, and Pat thought he should probably start taking it easy. I instantly agreed with her – animal welfare is always my top priority, and even without seeing Hugo I knew if his owner had even the tiniest concern he shouldn't be working any more. And that of course ruled out any further *Harry Potter* madness.

'I'm so sorry to let you down, Julie,' Pat had told me on the phone. 'I know it's so close to filming, but it's only recently that I've noticed any change in him.'

I reassured her that she had done exactly the right thing – there's no way I would ever want to do anything that put our lovely Hugo at risk.

For me, the health and happiness of the animal actors comes above everything else, and they all deserve a peaceful retirement when the time comes. But it did mean we had to find a replacement dog – and quickly.

Jo sank into a battered swivel chair, taking the news in. 'We're going to have to act fast to find another one, then,' she said. 'Time is not on our side.'

I nodded. That's exactly what had kept me rooted to this spot since I got off the phone to Pat.

Usually, if I was starting from scratch with a new dog I'd want at least twelve weeks working with them before taking them on set, starting by simply building a relationship before moving on to simple commands and eventually the specific moves they'd need for the film. *The Goblet of Fire* started in less than half that time. Fang's scenes weren't among the first to be shot, but even so, once filming started I'd have my hands full, so it was vital to begin the basics with a new dog before then.

I was well aware of the scale of the challenge. Neapolitan mastiffs are a rare breed, with only about 120 puppies registered in the UK every year. And they are also quite tricky dogs to work with. While there are always exceptions, breed has a big influence on a dog's personality. Common traits will depend on why the breed was originally developed – for example, toy dogs bred to sit in aristocratic ladies' laps generally enjoy a good cuddle, while terriers used to chase foxes and rabbits down holes love to dig. Mastiffs were guard dogs, and in my experience they tend to be wary of strangers, exhibiting guarding behaviour and sometimes acting aggressively.

Hugo himself had been a naturally suspicious dog, but over the course of three films and lots of training he had become a joy to work with. He had got much friendlier over time – perhaps too friendly on some occasions. I smiled as I remembered when we had taken him on ITV's *This Morning* show and he had given a very slobbery greeting to the presenter Fern Britton, leaving her absolutely covered in drool.

'You know, it was Gary who found Hugo,' I said to Jo. 'But it will be up to me this time.'

Gary Gero was the Hollywood trainer who had given me my first big break by hiring me as the head dog trainer on *101 Dalmatians* in 1995. Back then, I had just started to establish myself as a freelance trainer, having spent years trying to break into the business any way I could.

I had started from the bottom – even offering to clean dog kennels and animal cages for free in the hope of getting a job at an animal acting agency – and Gary was the one who recognised my potential. I had him to thank for introducing me to *Harry Potter.*

His US-based Birds & Animals Unlimited had won the animal contract for the first movie, which we filmed in 2000. He brought me on board, along with Jo, and together we worked on *Harry Potter and the Philosopher's Stone* and *Harry Potter and the Chamber of Secrets*. Then, in 2003, Gary put me in charge of the British arm of his business, Birds & Animals UK, which I was now running independently. Fang was one of the biggest animal parts in the films, and this time it would be my responsibility, not Gary's, to find the right dog.

'You know exactly where to start!' said Jo. She flipped open the laptop and loaded up Google, tapping 'Neapolitan Mastiff Rescue UK' into the search box.

'Look, there's a whole mastiff rescue organisation. Why don't you give them a call? Forget about owl training for the rest of the day – I'll take care of it.'

I felt a rush of affection for Jo, who always knew the right thing to do. She is so organised and practical – it was one of the first things I had admired about her when we met on *102*

Dalmatians. But she is also passionate about animals, especially giving deserving rescues a second chance of happiness – just as I am.

'Thanks, love,' I smiled. 'I'll get cracking. Good luck with the owls . . .'

Jo squeezed my shoulder as she headed for the door, and I turned back to the laptop. The breed's dedicated rescue group was definitely the place to start.

I always tried to cast rescue animals for movies because there are so many deserving animals languishing in shelters who are desperate for a new life. It breaks my heart to think of the cruelty and neglect humans can inflict on animals, but no matter what horrors a creature has endured, a bit of kindness and some careful training can turn them into stars. The world writes them off, but I knew from experience that rescues are often the hardest working, most loyal and loving animals. In fact, my first project in charge of Birds & Animals UK had involved an incredible rescue, which you can read about in my book *Will You Take Me Home?* Pickles the Yorkshire terrier had suffered unimaginable cruelty as a breeding dog on a puppy farm, but had gone on to blow everyone away as the star of the teen movie *What a Girl Wants.* Pickles was still my beloved pet and she had repaid the love I showed her in spades.

I scrolled through the Mastiff Rescue UK website until I found a phone number. With some trepidation, I dialled the number and crossed my fingers. Would they have what I was looking for?

I got through to a friendly woman called Debbie. I think she thought it was a prank when I first told her I was calling from the set of *Harry Potter*, looking for a dog who could play Fang. After I had reassured her that I really was who I said I was, she had some bad news for me.

'You know, I really would love to help,' she said. 'For us mastiff lovers it was such a thrill when you chose to use a Neapolitan in the film. I don't think many people had seen one before you made the breed famous! But I just don't have any Neos on the books at the moment.'

'That's OK,' I said, trying to keep the disappointment out of my voice. 'Will you keep me posted, in case you do hear of one that needs a home?'

'Of course!' said Debbie. 'Do you have a particular colour in mind?'

'Actually no,' I said. 'Any will do – we can work around it.' Hugo was 'blue', which is actually a dark grey, but believe it or not we often dye dogs' fur using a special animal-friendly product. On *101* and *102 Dalmatians* we even painted on extra spots to make their coats match when we had more than one dog playing the same role.

Debbie wrote down my details. 'I'll keep my ear to the ground, Julie,' she told me. 'You'll be the first to know.'

I hung up the phone, my heart sinking with disappointment. This was going to be even harder than I thought.

Chapter Three

The Search Continues

Reaching into my desk drawer, I pulled out the battered Filofax where I kept the numbers of all the animal shelters and dog charities I dealt with. Working methodically, I dialled number after number, and found myself greeted fondly by my contacts, who all wanted updates on the cats and dogs they had supplied me with over the years. I loved to chat with my old acquaintances – in my experience, people who work in animal rescue are among the kindest and most big hearted in the world – but when we got on to the question I had rung to ask, the answer was always the same. No, they didn't have a Neapolitan mastiff, but yes, they'd let me know if they heard of one.

The afternoon flew by and before I knew it, 5 p.m. had arrived. The shelters would be shutting for the night, and besides, I had pretty much exhausted my little black book. If only I was looking for a Staffordshire bull terrier or a lurcher, I thought. These poor dogs make up a huge proportion of those in rescue centres – unfairly, as they usually make excellent pets.

Deciding to call it a day, I hurried outside to the paddocks, hoping to catch the owl trainers before they clocked off. At last, I found something to make me smile. Five beautiful birds swooping in big circles in unison, while the trainers whooped with delight below. We were making progress here at least.

'No joy?' asked Jo, coming to join me where I

was leaning against the fence, watching the team in action.

I sighed. 'It doesn't look like I'm going to find a rescue,' I said. 'So I'll try the breed club next, see if they can put me in touch with anyone who might be able to loan me a dog.'

Jo simply nodded, but I knew she understood my disappointment. There's nothing wrong with using loan dogs – Hugo had been one, after all. But it was often tricky asking someone to part with their beloved pet for months on end and I really like working with rescues – the chance to give a deserving animal a second chance is one of the reasons I do this job. But with such a narrow time frame, I didn't really have many other options. I'd have to hope that the breed club would be able to help me find a dog, and one that was right for the movie. An added complication is that not all animals are cut out for training and filming. I was looking for a dog with lots of energy, a bold nature and a good appetite. I didn't mind if they were a bit naughty because that can be a good thing – cheeky dogs love having their mind busy, so thrive when they are trained. With lots of children on set, I also needed a dog that was relaxed around kids. It's not always a given.

I could feel my thoughts running away from me and I tried to snap myself out of my worry spiral. I had to stay optimistic: there was no point in panicking. I forced myself to focus on the team, who were high-fiving each other on the day's success.

'Great work, everyone,' I congratulated them. 'It's looking fab!'

As the trainers took the owls back to the aviary for their well-deserved dinner, I popped to the office to grab my laptop and lock up before heading home.

I had just switched the light off and had the keys in the door when the phone rang. My hands full with my papers and computer, I was tempted to leave it. But what if it was someone calling with a lead on a Neapolitan mastiff?

I hurried back to the desk, dumping my stuff on the chair, and grabbed the receiver before it rang out.

'Hello?' I said. I was surprised to hear it was Debbie from Mastiff Rescue UK. I hadn't been expecting her to call back so soon.

'Hi Julie, you won't believe this, but I just got off the phone and started chatting to my colleague about what you were after, and she told me she literally just took a call this morning about a new Neo. We haven't met him yet, but he's young and a bit of a handful apparently. His owner dropped him off at a pet rescue centre saying he's aggressive. The centre seems to think he will need specialist attention, so they've asked us to get involved.

'We're picking him up this evening – would you be interested in taking a look?'

My head was spinning. This dog was exactly

the breed I was looking for, but if he was aggressive, also not at all what I had in mind. Was this fate – or just a dead end?

Chapter Four

Out with the Old, In with the Neo

The Neapolitan mastiff was all I could think about as I drove home that evening.

A dangerous dog was not going to be right for a film set full of children. In twelve weeks' time I needed to present a dog that was calm, well trained and, crucially, friendly – and this might be one challenge too far. But we only had the owner's word for what the dog's temperament was like, so I knew I had to see for myself.

'I wouldn't rule him out,' Debbie had told me on the phone. 'Often owners say their mastiff is aggressive as an excuse to get rid of them. But nine times out of ten it's because they weren't prepared for how big the dog got or how expensive it is to feed them. People prefer to blame the dog than blame themselves.'

Hoping she was right, I had agreed that I'd be there to see the dog first thing the next morning. With the clock ticking, I couldn't afford not to follow up any possible lead. All I could do was hope his reputation was undeserved.

I took the turn for my village, Long Marston, and felt my body relax as my pretty cottage, with its wisteria-covered walls, came into view. It was always a delight to see it after a long day at the studios, knowing my loyal menagerie would be waiting for me inside. Some were working or retired film dogs – like Pickles the Yorkshire terrier, George and Ginelli the boxers and Gypsy, my white poodle. Then there was Lala – my crazy

Dalmatian who I had taken on in the hope she would work on *101 Dalmatians*, only to find she was completely unsuited to the task. And I also had the cats I was currently training for *Harry Potter*: Max, the enormous tabby who played Mrs Norris, and Crackerjack, the ginger Persian who played Crookshanks.

While I was putting in long days training or on set I had one of my team, who we call animal maintenance, come and exercise the dogs and socialise the cats on the days they weren't at the studios. Today it had been Lisa, who was relatively new to the company. I knew she always went above and beyond with the animals, so I expected the dogs to be worn out, having had lots of long walks and games.

Even so, my pets were still over the moon when I walked through the door. It's one of the reasons I've always loved animals so much – the joy they show at merely being in your presence is enough to make you feel like the most special person in the world. Little Pickles was bouncing around in happy circles of delight, while Lala tore around trying to bring me her toys all at once and Gypsy yapped with excitement. Red Ginelli was jumping up while George, white with a big brown patch over one eye, nudged my hand with his warm snout, desperate for a stroke.

'Hello babies,' I greeted them warmly, trying to give them all a fuss at once. 'Did you miss me?' I scooped Pickles up in my arms and the others followed to my squashy red sofa, where we collapsed in a doggy heap. 'It's good to be home,' I told them.

My mobile pinged with a text message. I picked it up and smiled to see it was from Glenn, my boyfriend. 'Heading your way!' he wrote. 'Do you want anything from the shop? Besides the essentials (chocolate and wine).'

'Those are definitely essential today!' I typed back. 'Can't wait to see you xx.'

Glenn and I had been dating for just over six

months, and I felt like I was falling more in love with him every day. He was one of the first people I met after I moved to Long Marston the previous year, and at first we were just friends. When we finally plucked up the courage to tell each other how we felt, I knew straight away that it would be serious. These days he spent more time at my cottage than he did at his own barn conversion down the road, despite the fact he was constantly battling his allergies to my many animals.

'Enjoy your spot on the sofa while it lasts, kids,' I told the dogs, who were making themselves comfy. 'Glenn's on his way, so you'll have to budge up.'

He arrived fifteen minutes later and I straight away told him what was on my mind: the loss of Hugo and having to source a new Neapolitan mastiff.

'They're tricky dogs, you see,' I told him, taking the bottle of red out of his shopping bag and pouring two big glasses. 'We had it cracked with Hugo but I'm just not sure how easy it's going to be with a new one, and in such a tight time frame.'

'All right, all right,' Glenn said, fending off Lala, who always tried to enlist him in a game of tug of war. 'Let's just pause a minute. Can I have a hug from my girlfriend?'

I smiled, and leaned in to his open arms. He was taller than me, with light brown hair and strong arms from his job selling oak furniture. 'Sorry, Glenn,' I said. 'Just a lot on my mind.'

'I know,' he said, looking down at me with his twinkly blue eyes. 'But you'll sort it – you always do.'

Glenn threw together a quick dinner of pasta and pesto and filled me in on his day while I got on with the complicated task of feeding the animals their specially planned, nutritionally balanced meals. Lisa always left a note of how many treats the dogs had been given during the day so I could adjust their dinner accordingly.

'You've been a greedy guts again, then, Ginelli,' I murmured as he looked up at me with a butter-wouldn't-melt expression.

After we'd all eaten, I was drying up when my phone pinged again. It was a text from Debbie.

'Just picked up dog,' it read. 'Not in gr8 state. But you def shd see him.'

I felt my heart sink. My expectations were already low, but it sounded like things were worse than I realised. If he was in a bad state, he may have been mistreated, which could explain his aggression. Was there any chance this poor dog could ever play Fang? And if so, would I have enough time to train him?

Chapter Five

Rescue Mission

The next morning, I was awake before Pickles – who slept at the foot of my bed and was more efficient than any alarm clock – had even stirred. I felt more optimistic now that it was a new day. Rescuing animals that had been abused and neglected was what I did best – why should this be any different?

I looked fondly at Pickles, her little tawny belly rising and falling gently as she snored at the end of the stripy duvet. She had been in a truly terrible state when she came to me from the puppy farm, her coat covered in mange, her ears crawling with mites and her little legs so weak she could barely keep herself upright. Now she was a perfect princess; one of the smartest dogs I had ever trained.

And animals that had experienced violence – hadn't I worked with animals before who proved that it didn't inevitably lead to aggression? I remembered one dog I trained who we feared had been beaten horrifically by his cruel owner before I got him, but he had the sweetest nature. I trusted him completely – he didn't have a bad bone in his body. With the right love and attention, this mastiff could still play Fang, whatever his background.

As if she could sense me watching her, Pickles sleepily opened her eyes. When she saw I was awake she wriggled excitedly up to the head of the bed, squeezing herself in between Glenn, still fast asleep, and me. I smiled and stroked her soft ears. 'Wish me luck today,' I whispered.

When you have as many animals as I do, you don't get much chance for a lie-in. After half an hour dozing with Pickles curled on my chest, it was time to get up. Glenn joined me as we took the dogs for a brisk walk through the woods behind my cottage to the meadow, where the cherry trees were starting to blossom. Here we threw balls for the dogs and watched them gallop around. Then Glenn kissed me good-bye as he headed back to his own place to get ready for work.

I returned to the cottage, where I had the hectic task of getting breakfast for the dogs and the two cats, then making sure they ate their own and didn't steal anyone else's. Lala in particular was always trying to pinch some of Gypsy's, although I had never seen her actually succeed – Gypsy was tougher than she looked.

The dogs were just finishing up when there was a knock at the door. It was Lisa, who had come to look after the animals while I headed up to Nottinghamshire to meet Debbie and the Neapolitan mastiff.

'Hi Julie!' she beamed. 'Sorry I'm a bit early!'

Only Lisa would apologise for being on time. Petite, with her red hair cut in a bob, she was already an essential part of my working life. Having someone like her to depend on while I was tearing all over the country made life so much easier. It felt like she'd been working with us for ever, when in fact she had only started a few months ago.

'Don't be silly,' I told her as she followed me into the cottage.

I had met Lisa through one of my neighbours, who had told me how animal-mad his niece was. She was working at a petting farm but would love a job at my company, he said. When he described Lisa, I was reminded of my younger self, working at a dog-grooming parlour in Harrow, where I grew up, but desperate to break into the movie business.

I told my neighbour to give Lisa my number, and a few days later she came up to the farm on the edge of the village, which I use as a training ground. That day I had her doing all sorts of odd jobs, from mucking out the owl pens to taking the dogs for their lunchtime run and grooming the llama we had just taken on. I was immediately impressed by her sweet nature and dedication to the animals, and by the end of the day I had offered her a full-time job.

'So, it's just the usual today, Lisa,' I told her as I led her into the kitchen and the dogs all started going mad, excited to see one of their favourite people. 'I'm not going to the set, though, so I might be back a bit later than normal. Is that OK?'

'Of course it is,' said Lisa, looking up at me from the floor where she was crouching, giving George a belly rub. 'What are you doing instead?'

'I'm hoping to find a new Fang,' I replied. 'Hugo has had to retire, so we need a replacement, and there's a charity up in Nottinghamshire that has a potential Neapolitan mastiff.'

'How exciting!' grinned Lisa. 'I can't wait to meet him – I love big dogs like that.'

I smiled, knowing I could rely on her to keep my dogs happy and healthy while I was away. 'Just as well,' I said. 'I'm going to need plenty of help if I bring him home.'

As Lisa took the dogs into the garden to play, I put a lead and a harness for a large dog in the back of my Mitsubishi Shogun. The car was specially adapted so I could safely carry several animals at once in separate crates. I was about to close the boot when I decided I should probably take out some of the bars from the top and side of one of the crates so it was big enough for a tall, bulky dog. If I was lucky and the Neo was coming home with me, chances were he'd be too big to comfortably travel in a regular-height crate.

I called goodbye to Lisa, then put the address

of Debbie's charity into my satnav. I could feel butterflies building in my stomach as I eased the car out of the driveway. Would the dog be right for the film – and would the film be right for him? It was time to find out.

Chapter Six

Hello Hercules

I arrived at Mastiff Rescue UK a little before lunch. I knew they rehomed mastiffs – not just Neapolitans, but other breeds like bullmastiffs, English mastiffs and Tibetan mastiffs too. The mastiff family is made up of majestic, muscular breeds which are among the oldest known to humans. Over the centuries they've been used not just as guard dogs but as fighting animals and even dogs of war.

English mastiffs, sometimes known simply as

mastiffs, are the biggest of the bunch – males growing to at least 76cm tall. They've been around since Roman times, when they were used to fight human gladiators, bears, bulls, lions and tigers for the entertainment of the nobility.

Bullmastiffs, with a shorter muzzle and black face, were used by nineteenth-century game-keepers to guard England's great estates against poachers. They are known as the 'silent watch-dog' because they are quieter than other mastiff breeds, relying instead on their sheer size and strength to see off intruders.

Then there's the Tibetan mastiff, a mountain dog with a heavy, shaggy coat and an extremely independent mind. They're intelligent and super-protective, but that coat certainly takes a lot of grooming!

Finally, the Neapolitan mastiff, with its distinc-tive wrinkly skin and heavy jowls. As the name suggests, they were developed in Italy as guard dogs and can be fearsome when they want to be.

Thanks to their massive size and idiosyncratic personalities, mastiffs aren't for everyone. Mastiff Rescue UK took dogs either direct from owners who couldn't cope any more or from rescue centres around the country who wanted the charity to use their expertise and network of contacts to find a loving new owner. Usually they would foster them out with their team of mastiff-loving volunteers until a permanent home was found.

The dog I had come to see was one of those who had been passed to them via a regular dog shelter. I had very few details of his background from Debbie, so I would have to see what else I could find out.

The rescue centre indicated that Mastiff Rescue UK was a homespun affair. It was basically a farmhouse, smartly painted white with big picture windows. I could see well-kept barns beyond a neat farmyard, which I assumed acted as kennels for the dogs. The place was spotless, and I could already sense that this was an organisation that didn't compromise. I knocked on the door of the main house, my anticipation growing.

'Julie?' said the tall woman with closely cropped grey hair who answered.

I smiled. 'Hi! You must be Debbie.'

Debbie gave me a robust handshake. 'Thanks for coming at such short notice. I hope Hercules will be what you're looking for – he could really do with a lovely home.'

So that was his name: Hercules. It sounded very grand.

'I'll take you straight round,' said Debbie, stepping outside and shutting the door behind her. 'One of our volunteers, Mearsy, is giving him some exercise now. Try not to be alarmed by what he looks like – Hercules, that is, not Mearsy!'

I liked Debbie already: there was something commanding about her presence and I could see how she must be good with these powerful, bullish breeds. Although many mastiffs are gentle giants, they are immensely big and strong, so they need a firm hand.

Debbie led me past the barns – peering in, I saw I was right about them being dog accommodation. There were no dogs in there so they must all have been out for exercise or maybe lounging inside the farmhouse, but I could see comfy beds and lots of toys in the spacious pens.

'This is where we keep the dogs when they first come to us,' Debbie said. 'But I don't think a kennel is a very natural place for most dogs, so we try to get them into homes as soon as possible. Often it turns out to be my house before we find them a more permanent home – I always say there's room for one more!'

My gut instinct had been correct – this was a place where animal welfare was paramount. Debbie was clearly devoted to her rescue mission.

Beyond the barns was a paddock, where I could see the back of Mearsy, a thickset man of about sixty in a heavy overcoat. He was whistling to the dog, who I couldn't quite see yet because of how the paddock was banked.

Then, all of a sudden, Hercules came into view. He didn't exactly take after his Roman god name-sake, though: he was more like Scooby-Doo. Lanky and gangly, he was galloping towards Mearsy, a ball clamped in his enormous jaws. I couldn't help but giggle at how clumsy and crazy he was.

But as he came closer, I took a sharp intake of breath. I suddenly understood why Debbie had warned me Hercules wasn't in a good state. He was incredibly skinny – little more than a bag of bones. A Neapolitan mastiff should have skin that hangs loose over the solid rock of their body, but this dog's folds were like old rags draped around his bony frame. I felt a stab in my heart when I realised how he must have been starved and neglected by his former owners.

'Mearsy!' called Debbie. 'The movie trainer's here – bring him over to say hello.'

Turning round, Mearsy gave me a wide smile

which flashed two gold teeth. 'Come on then, boy,' he said to Hercules, clipping a lead on to him. When Hercules spotted Debbie and me waiting at the paddock gate, he suddenly started straining towards us with excitement, almost pulling poor Mearsy off his feet.

'Here he is, then,' said Mearsy, his face red from the exertion of trying to keep the enormous dog under control. 'What do you think?'

Hercules was still straining towards me and I reached out my hand towards him so he could have a sniff. He was full of slobbery delight at seeing me, the trails of drool, common to a lot of mastiffs, giving him a comical expression. Hercules might have been too skinny, but I could tell he would be an exceedingly handsome boy once he put on a bit of weight. His coat was the perfect shade of thundery grey, like clouds before a storm. His shoulders were wide and strapping, and his deep-set brown eyes sparkled with alertness.

Sensing Hercules was happy for me to do so, I tickled him behind his ears. He looked up at me with a look of such gentleness that I immediately knew that whatever I had heard about his aggressive side must be wrong. I could tell this was a dog who just longed to be loved.

'Hi, boy,' I murmured softly. Sometimes you just feel an instant connection with an animal, and this was one of those occasions. All thoughts of *Harry Potter* vanished from my mind, as I gently stroked Hercules' floppy ears. This poor dog, so desperately malnourished, deserved love and attention – and I knew I wouldn't be able to resist taking him home to get him well.

Chapter Seven

A Blank Slate

Hercules tilted his head to one side, as if he could understand what I was thinking, and I just knew he and I would be a great team.

Debbie was smiling, watching us. 'I thought you'd love him,' she said. 'He's a real sweetheart.'

I stroked Hercules' velvety head, and he leaned into me happily. 'He doesn't seem the aggressive type,' I commented. An aggressive dog would not have been so keen to seek affection from an unknown human, and would have approached in a much more guarded way. Hercules couldn't have been more relaxed.

Mearsy made a sound of annoyance. 'It's typical,' he said. 'So many owners who ditch their mastiffs say they are aggressive, and as you can see, it's often a lie.' I could tell he was a true mastiff lover, and he was taking the falsehood about Hercules personally.

Debbie nodded. 'Apparently, he was brought to the rescue centre by a man who wouldn't give his name. Claimed the dog was his mate's but the guys at the rescue centre reckon he was probably the owner. He insisted the dog was aggressive and couldn't be kept at home any more. But I think the story is probably a bit more complicated than that.'

I had to agree with Debbie's suspicions. I ran my hands gently over Hercules' long back and could feel his knobbly spine and every one of his ribs. His previous owners hadn't been feeding him properly, and going by the state of his coat, which was balding in places on his leg and belly, he hadn't been housed properly either. I would guess he'd been shut outside and ignored, which for a dog as affectionate as him would have been pure torture – and that's before you factor in the cruel winter weather we'd just endured.

'It sounds like the poor boy's been through the mill,' I said. 'But I know I can give him a very happy new life. I'll get him healthy first, then try him with the training. Whether or not he takes to it will determine if I continue, but either way I will make sure he has a loving home for as long as he lives.' I meant it too: no animal I took on would ever have less than the best. It didn't matter if he made the movie or not, I would get this dog healthy and ensure he had the happy home he deserved.

I glanced up and saw that Mearsy looked pretty emotional. His voice cracked slightly as he handed me the lead and rubbed Hercules' head for the final time. 'This dog deserves nothing less,' he managed, then stomped away towards the barns.

Debbie shook her head, smiling. 'Poor Mearsy always gets so attached to the dogs, even if they've only been here a day, like Hercules.'

I knew how he felt. Over the years I've worked with more animals than I can count, but each and every one was special to me. You might not get to keep them all, but the memories will always be precious.

'It's actually unusual for us to identify a potential new home so quickly,' Debbie went on. 'As I say, we don't know too much about his background, but I'll do my best to answer any questions you have.'

'Do you know how old he is?' I asked, sizing Hercules up again. 'And if he's had any training whatsoever?' I reckoned he wasn't much more than a puppy and it seemed unlikely his neglect-ful owners had spent much time on training if they couldn't even be bothered to feed him.

'We think he's about a year old, possibly as much as eighteen months,' Debbie replied. 'He's probably as tall as he's going to get but will obviously fill out more, especially when he's eating right.

'He seems to be toilet trained, but I don't think he knows many commands. We've tried recall and sit but he doesn't respond to either. So I'm afraid you'd be working from scratch.'

I nodded. 'That's OK,' I said. 'A blank slate isn't a bad thing. And he's still young so he should pick up training fairly fast. That's if he takes to it, of course – like I said, it's his welfare that really matters to me, not the movie.'

Debbie beamed. 'Well, I think you and him will be the perfect fit. If you're keen to take him, shall we get the paperwork sorted?'

'Yes please,' I told her. 'I'd love to take him home with me.'

I followed Debbie back up to the farmhouse, Hercules yanking my arm from side to side as he excitedly sniffed everything he could reach on the way. Inside the house, the kitchen was like a shrine to mastiffs, with framed photographs of dogs covering every inch of the walls. Three noble-looking English mastiffs, with their typical fawn coats and black faces, sprawled across the tiled floor, making it a bit of an obstacle course for Hercules and me to pick our way to the kitchen table – especially as Hercules was beside himself with excitement at coming face to face with new dogs. They mostly ignored him, barely stirring from their snoozes.

Debbie offered me a cup of tea, and when it came, it was in a mug that read 'Mastiff Mummy'.

'I suppose you could say I'm a bit obsessed,' she smiled, clocking me looking from the mug to the photos on the walls.

I grinned. 'Nothing wrong with that!'

Debbie took a sip of tea and handed me the adoption contracts to read through. 'Mastiffs are just very misunderstood dogs,' she said. 'But they can be so rewarding. I'd say Hercules will be a case in point – I've only had him about twenty-four hours, but I can already tell he's a really loving boy.'

I looked down at Hercules' eager face. I realised he had barely taken his eyes off me, as if imploring me not to ignore him. And how could I, when he was such a gorgeous little soul? I patted his head gently, feeling a rush of love for this awkward misfit, and he shuffled his skinny body even closer to me.

'I reckon you're right,' I said, picking up a pen to sign the documents. 'But I can tell it's going to be a bit of a challenge . . .'

'Oh, definitely,' Debbie nodded. 'He's going to need some help getting fighting fit. And he's pretty much at square one when it comes to training. But that's why I'm so pleased he's going with you – he needs someone experienced, and you seem like the woman for the job.' She paused, as if deciding whether to reveal something. 'I looked you up online,' she finally added. 'It's really impressive, what you do – I think Hercules is very lucky to have found you.'

I blushed: even after years in the business I still got impostor syndrome and didn't think anything I did was that special. I had to hope I wouldn't let Debbie down – and more importantly, I wouldn't let Hercules down either.

Chapter Eight

Monkey Business

Before I loaded Hercules into the car, I wanted to take some photos to record how skinny he was. I would hate to have an animal in my care looking like that and people thinking I was responsible.

Debbie agreed to try to hold him still while I took some snaps with the digital camera I had brought with me. It proved quite the challenge. Hercules was like a big puppy, constantly trying to jump up at Debbie to lick her face or dart towards me or roll on his back with his enormous legs flailing in the air.

'Training can't start soon enough!' I laughed, after I had finally got enough shots that showed his jutting hips and visible ribcage. I was pleased to see that his low weight hadn't left him lethargic and subdued, but he was certainly an unruly customer.

There was something niggling at the back of my mind, though. 'Hercules' just didn't suit this big floppy goofball at all. That name was too serious, too noble – adjectives you certainly wouldn't use to describe this dog.

Debbie walked us to my car, Hercules still straining at his lead and nearly wrenching my arm out of its socket.

'So, just one final question,' I said. 'How attached is he to the name "Hercules"?'

Debbie laughed. 'I know what you're thinking – doesn't suit him at all, does it?' she said. 'It was the name the man who dropped him off at the rescue centre gave. But to be honest, I think he's been so neglected I'm not sure he recognises it as his own – he certainly doesn't come when you call him. So you could definitely change it if you want to.'

'Great,' I grinned. 'I'll let you know what I decide on.'

I opened the back of the car and helped Hercules climb in, and he immediately started trying to climb out again. 'Whoa, boy,' I laughed, gently but firmly pushing him back in and getting him settled. 'No monkey business, please.'

Debbie and I shook hands. 'Good luck,' she said heartily. 'I'll be following his career with interest – let me know if he makes the cut for *Harry Potter*.'

'I really hope he will,' I replied as I got into the car. And with a wave, Hercules and I were off.

I soon realised it would not be an easy journey. Hercules quickly noticed I'd taken out some of the bars to give him the space he needed – and was already making an escape attempt.

'Hey, Houdini, get back there!' I yelled, trying to keep my eyes on the road even though I could see in the rear-view mirror that Hercules was slithering his enormous body over the top of the crate and onto the back seat.

The next thing I knew, a big wet nose was nudging my hand on the gearstick as he shoved his bulky head through the gap between the front seats.

I pulled over, thanking my lucky stars it was a deserted country road. Hercules, delighted we had stopped, immediately shimmied through an unfeasibly small gap and tumbled onto the passenger seat, then lolled his head into my lap. I had to laugh, despite his naughtiness. There was something irresistible about his uncontainable urge to be as close to you as possible.

'You are a not-so-little monkey,' I told him. Reaching behind me for his lead, I clipped it back on and encouraged him out of the car. I took him for a quick stroll up and down the road, trying to get rid of some of his excess energy. I've met plenty of rescues who are nervous around people or take a long time to come out of their shell. Hercules wasn't one of them.

I tied him to the back of the car while I fiddled around with the configuration of the crate bars, until I had something I knew would be safe and secure. I had thought my earlier efforts would be enough, but I hadn't banked on the ingenuity of Hercules.

'Right, this time, stay put please,' I told him. He hopped in, but I could tell by the giddy look on his face he wasn't ready to settle.

I got back into the driver's seat and we pulled away. Glancing in the rear-view mirror, I could see Hercules pawing at the bars, trying to find a way out. It was all a big game to him. He snuffled around for a bit, then rolled onto his side, then gave an excited yelp.

'Not long, boy,' I told him. 'We'll be home soon, and then we can play.'

Hercules paused while I spoke, but as soon as I turned my eyes back to the road, he gave a deep bark. Then another, and another. 'It's going to be a long journey if you keep that up,' I said, keeping my voice light-hearted. It didn't have any effect. Hercules had settled into his barking now, deep, throaty booms that made the whole car vibrate.

'I can see you're going to be a handful,' I said. There was no point getting annoyed – he was just a dog, doing what dogs do. 'My silly monkey.'

Calling him a monkey again got my mind whirring. It was the perfect nickname for a dog this daft and cheeky. So why not make it his real name too?

'Monkey!' I called out over his barks. 'How do you like that? Shall we call you Monkey?' And, just like that, he paused. I thought he was gearing up for another round of barking, but instead he finally quietened down and settled himself on his belly.

So that was it: goodbye Hercules, hello Monkey. I readied myself for plenty of Monkey madness ahead.

Chapter Nine

Weight Watchers

I wasn't taking Monkey straight home – I wanted to get him checked over at the vet's first. The previous evening I had called Michelle, my vet at Wendover Heights surgery, to warn her I might be bringing a new charge to see her the following afternoon. 'I look forward to your next challenge!' she had told me on the phone.

Having treated my animals for several years, Michelle knew what to expect. I would often turn up at her door with rescues for whom I had very little backstory, hoping that she could fill in the blanks and help me get them healthy. For her part, Michelle was always calm and kind no matter what problem I threw at her, and as dedicated to the welfare of my animals as I am. I knew I could rely on her, and always trusted her judgement.

As I predicted, Monkey was giddy to find himself in a vet's waiting room full of lots of other cats and dogs, as well as a few crates inside which hid shy hamsters and rabbits. I wasn't sure how he would be with other animals yet so I kept my distance, choosing a plastic chair in a little alcove beneath a poster about how often you should worm your dog. It took all my strength to keep Monkey safely by my side, such was his determination to head into the main part of the waiting room and investigate the snuffling, twitching and whining patients there.

'Julie?' Michelle emerged from her examination room. She was just a few years younger than me, about thirty-two, with short curly brown hair she wore neatly tucked behind her ears.

'Hi Michelle,' I said, standing up and immediately finding myself lurched forwards by Monkey, who was ploughing towards her, his tail wagging at a hundred miles an hour. 'Meet Monkey!'

Michelle crouched down to give Monkey a fuss and he lapped it up, his whole body wriggling in hyperactive joy. 'You're certainly full of beans, aren't you?' she said.

Inside Michelle's consulting room, lined with anatomy posters, Monkey gave a big shake, sending drool splattering up the walls. 'Oh, I'm sorry!' I said, reaching in my pocket for a tissue to try to clean Monkey up.

'Don't be silly, Jules,' smiled Michelle. 'Occupational hazard. You better get used to it with this one.'

I sighed gratefully and put the tissue away. The drool didn't bother me – it seemed a small price to pay for a dog who was so bouncy and loving – but I knew not everyone would feel the same.

'Well, as you can see, he's very underweight,' I said, getting straight to the point. 'But do you think he has any other health issues?'

'Hmm, he certainly is far too skinny,' said Michelle. I distracted Monkey with a handful of treats as she ran her hands over his painfully mal-nourished body, feeling every protruding bone. Under the bright lights in Michelle's consulting room, I could see exactly how thin he was, and I felt tears pricking at my eyes. How could anyone have let this happen to such a beautiful animal?

'His weight suggests he's been badly neglected,' she said. 'Big dogs like this have big appetites, and he's not been getting enough food – or the right food, judging by the state of his teeth and gums,' she added, peeling back his baggy lips.

Michelle peered into Monkey's eyes, then lifted up his massive floppy ears and inspected in there too. Then she reached for her syringe so she could take some blood samples. Still snuffling in my fist for the treats, Monkey barely noticed as she gently pressed the needle in. I hugged him close to me, breathing in his comforting doggy smell.

'Well, the good news is I can't see anything else immediately wrong with him,' she said. 'I'll get these blood samples sent off just to be sure, but he seems in fairly good shape otherwise. Once you get his diet right his coat won't be as dull and patchy either. I would say he'll have more energy too, but you don't seem to be having too many problems in that department.'

We both laughed as Monkey suddenly caught a glimpse of his own tail and tried to bounce after it, bashing into the legs of Michelle's examination table and giving it a good wobble in the process.

'It's quite amazing that he's so underfed but so full of life,' said Michelle. 'Usually dogs which are starving are weak and subdued; he's going to be quite a handful when he's firing on all cylinders.'

'Oh, I know,' I said ruefully. 'It's especially

unusual, because in my experience Neapolitan mastiffs are pretty lazy and chilled. Not this one – he's just an overgrown puppy!'

Together we hoisted Monkey onto the scales and Michelle tutted as she noted down his weight.

'We still need to take the same steps as we would with any malnourished dog,' Michelle said, scribbling on her pad. 'I know you know the drill, but just a reminder: small meals, little and often. A balance of wet and dry food. Don't let him gorge himself.'

Unfortunately, I had a fair amount of experience with looking after starved rescue animals and getting them back up to a healthy weight. It's the most basic requirement of a pet owner to keep your animal well fed, but so many neglect their responsibilities before dumping their animal in a horrendous state at a rehoming centre, or leaving them at death's door to be rescued by animal inspectors.

There are few things sadder than seeing an

animal which is dependent on humans for food going without, and their body wasting away. I knew that Monkey would have to eat a high-protein, low-carb diet so that he could quickly get the nutrients he needed without shocking his system. I would supplement it with Omega 3 and fatty acids, and minerals, to help his body recover from going without enough food for so long.

It seemed counterintuitive, but Monkey would have to eat small meals first because anything too big might cause him to vomit or prompt diarrhoea, which would be no good at all. We had to slowly and gently get him back on track in a way he could handle. Only if we were able to bring him back from the brink of starvation in a controlled and healthy way would I be able to properly start training him. It was a big if – because, despite his energy, Monkey was a seriously poorly dog.

'And I'm sure you'll be across this too, but you know how important it is to watch out for signs of bloat with a breed like this?' Michelle asked.

I nodded. I had worked with enough big dogs to know how dangerous the condition could be. Bloat is caused when too much gas builds up inside the dog, causing the stomach to twist. Once it happens, you have about twenty minutes to get the dog emergency treatment, or it's game over. Bloat literally kills, and is especially common in large breeds or dogs with deep chests – like a Neapolitan mastiff.

'All my staff are trained on what to look out for, but I'll be making sure I do a refresher now we've got Monkey on the books,' I told Michelle. The steps we took to prevent it included always resting the dogs for two hours after feeding, when bloat is most likely to occur.

'Great,' said Michelle. 'I know he's in good hands. I'll give you a ring if the tests throw anything up, and make sure you call me if you have any further concerns. Bring him back in a couple of weeks and we'll weigh him again, see how he's getting on.'

'Thanks, Michelle,' I said. I glanced in the paper bag she handed me, which contained some dietary supplements to help Monkey gain weight.

She showed us out and we headed back to the car. Monkey seemed to have exhausted himself with his antics at the vet's, and for the first time since we met he trotted calmly at my side. It was no wonder he was tired: with so few fat reserves, he was basically running on empty.

I felt a little exhausted myself – it had been an eventful day. I had gone to Nottinghamshire with low expectations and come home with this adorable handful who already had a very special place in my heart.

As usual, I felt a sense of trepidation, knowing a new rescue relied on me, but also excitement at the prospect of getting to know Monkey properly and giving him the care he needed. I had some patient, careful work ahead of me – and I absolutely had to get it right.

Chapter Ten

Food for Thought

Back in the car, I glanced at my watch. It was just after half past two, meaning training would still be in full swing at the studios. A plan was forming in my mind and I needed to run it by Jo. Plus I was keen for the other trainers to see our newest recruit.

'What do you think – shall we go and see your new office?' I asked Monkey. He grunted his assent. That was good enough for me. I turned right out of the vet's car park and made the familiar drive over to Leavesden. I was grateful Monkey had so quickly got used to being in the car – some dogs hate it, and struggle to settle.

When I arrived at the studios and parked up, it was deserted. I knew that meant the team would be in the far paddock, working with the owls. That suited me fine. I didn't want to overwhelm Monkey by introducing too many people to him at once. He seemed like such a good-natured, affectionate dog, but you can never make assumptions about rescue animals. You never know what triggers they might have or how they will react to unfamiliar situations. Monkey was a big, powerful beast, and it was important to respect that, no matter how soppy he seemed on the outside.

I took him round to the kennels where I knew we had all sorts of food stored. It was time to give him the first of his small, regular meals. I let him into the storeroom, lined with bins of feed and shelves groaning with animal toys, harnesses and leads. Then I unclipped his leash so he could have a sniff around while I made up his lunch.

I measured out two small scoops of high-protein dog food into a bowl, and added the mineral supplements. It looked like a measly portion, but I knew it was all Monkey would be able to safely manage right now.

I was so absorbed in my task that when I turned round, the bowl in my hands, I was surprised to see Monkey right there. I got even more of a shock to see how he was poised. Every one of his muscles was tense and his lips were pulled back, his teeth bared. Suddenly, he was lunging at me.

I immediately panicked. How had I misjudged the situation so badly? Here I was, on my own, with an enormous, potentially dangerous dog. I had taken it for granted that his previous owner had been lying about his aggressive side, but what if he had been right? There was no way I'd be able to fight off Monkey on my own: even though he was underweight, he was still a large dog, bred for guarding.

Then, almost as quickly as it had begun, the moment was over. Monkey didn't want to lunge at my throat as my instincts had imagined – he wanted the food and was bouncing up and down in front of me. I burst out into relieved laughter as I put the bowl on the floor, his face already in it. The poor creature was so hungry that once he saw food was on offer, he had not been able to control himself.

As I watched him inhale the small portion of food, I felt a heaviness in my heart for what Monkey had been through. Here was a dog desperate to be loved, who had been treated as if he was a complete irrelevance. His previous owners hadn't bothered to feed him properly, and if they couldn't even do that I knew they would not have given him the attention and affection he craved.

Despite the neglect, Monkey still had an admirable lust for life, and an open, loving nature.

Animals like him are the reason I keep coming back to rescues time and again. No matter what hardships and cruelty creatures like him endure, they still have an eagerness to please and capacity for love which I find deeply moving. Anything you give to an animal like Monkey, they will repay ten times over.

I was in love with this big silly lump of a dog already, but there was a problem. He needed a lot of space, and some one-on-one care – which I was going to find tricky, with my full-on schedule and the seven animals I already shared my little cottage with. I would, of course, be totally involved in his care and training, but he needed somewhere else to live. Which is what I wanted to talk to Jo about.

I always want the animals I train to be living as family pets, but I couldn't keep them all at home. Often, they lived with members of the animal maintenance team, who cared for them and loved them as if they were their own. The animals were still mine – I paid for all their food, their vet's bills, their insurance and everything else – and they would spend most of the day with me, working on training. But by living elsewhere it meant there was someone else to provide a steady presence at the end of the day, and lots of extra love and cuddles.

Having seen how Monkey was, I thought this would be the most appropriate solution. I would get to spend most of the day with him, but he needed some space of his own.

What I wanted to get Jo's opinion on was whether we should suggest that Lisa took him. She hadn't been working for us for very long, but I was so impressed by how gentle and patient she was with the animals. Lisa had said how much she loved big dogs, and something told me she would be the perfect foster mummy for Monkey.

Having licked every last morsel from the bowl – then licked it thoroughly again, just for good measure – Monkey padded over to where I was sitting on the storeroom's rickety old chair. He put his elephantine head in my lap and looked up at me with irresistible puppy-dog eyes. I smiled down at him, sorry that I had ever doubted his sweet nature.

'I shouldn't have misjudged you, boy,' I said, stroking his long ears. 'You were just so hungry, weren't you? Well, I promise you, you will never go hungry again.'

Monkey put his paw on my foot and leaned against me. In the short time we had been together I had noticed that whenever he could, he wanted some part of his body to be touching part of mine. It seemed to make him feel safe and secure, and it was a signal that he trusted me. I felt my heart swell. Already he and I were a little pack.

Reaching into my pocket for my phone, I texted Jo. 'At the studios, in storeroom. Come on your next break – someone I'd like you to meet.'

Chapter Eleven

Foster Mum

I didn't have to wait long before I heard Jo's footsteps hurrying along the corridor of the kennels. She rapped lightly on the storeroom door, giving me time to clip Monkey back onto the lead. I wanted to make sure he wouldn't knock her over in his eagerness to say hello.

'Come in!' I called. Jo flung the door open and, as predicted, Monkey started going mad with excitement, straining towards her.

'Well, what a handsome boy!' cried Jo. 'How is

he with people?' she said as she held her hand out for Monkey to have a sniff.

'Oh, well, you can probably see he's a people person,' I laughed. Jo grinned and bent down to give Monkey a fuss, trying to avoid his most slobbery kisses. I smiled fondly, feeling like a proud mum to my new baby.

'What happened to this terrifying problem mutt I thought you were picking up?' joked Jo. She knew as well as me that there is very rarely such a thing as a bad dog – just a bad owner.

'A happy twist of fate,' I smiled. 'I don't want to get ahead of myself, but he's so much better than I could have imagined. If he's like this with kids and other animals too, we're laughing.'

Jo nodded, but I could see her taking in his skinny frame. 'Definitely needs fattening up,' she said. 'What are you calling him?'

I grimaced. 'Well, his previous owners called him Hercules—'

'Oh God, no!' said Jo, outraged. 'That doesn't

suit him at all.' I stifled a giggle. This was why I loved Jo – we were always on exactly the same page.

'I know,' I said. 'So I've already changed it. What do you think of Monkey?'

'Monkey,' Jo repeated to herself. 'Monkey . . . yes, that will do nicely. Are you ready to be a movie star, Monkey?' In response he rolled happily onto his back, begging for a belly rub.

'We've obviously got some work to do to put weight on him,' I said. 'Michelle reckons he's badly malnourished. But he's still got plenty of energy, so hopefully we'll be able to see how he does with training fairly quickly. The focus has to be on getting him well, though.'

I hoped that I could start some very gentle preliminary training while I got some weight on Monkey over the next three weeks. If he took to it, then I would still have plenty of time to train him properly before Fang's first scenes. I'd be juggling training and filming with the other animals too, of course, but if I needed to put in extra hours to get Monkey up to speed then that's what I'd do.

'For sure,' said Jo, still crouched on the floor with Monkey. 'Are you thinking of taking him home with you?'

'Well, this is what I want to talk to you about,' I said. 'I'm not sure I've got the room. He's such a big boy. So, I was thinking of asking Lisa to take him. What do you reckon?'

Jo looked up at me, beaming. 'That's a perfect idea!' she said. 'Lisa will do a wonderful job, and I know she'll love having him.'

It was what I was hoping Jo would say. 'You think she's ready then?' I asked.

'Oh definitely!' said Jo. 'You've seen how amazing she is with your dogs, and she's had plenty of animals of her own. She knows what to do.'

'Well, we just have to hope she says yes, then!' I smiled, reaching for my phone.

Lisa picked up on the second ring. 'Hi Julie, is

everything all right?' I could hear Gypsy's unmistakable yaps in the background, and knew she must be on a walk with my little pack.

'Yes, all fine,' I said. 'But there's something I need to ask you – in person. Where are you now?'

'I've just got to the reservoirs,' Lisa replied. 'I'll be here for about an hour, I reckon.'

'OK, great, I'll meet you there,' I said, and hung up. I wanted Lisa to see Monkey for herself before she decided whether to take him on. After all, while I adored him already I knew that many people would see a dog who was big and slobbery and unruly – not the easiest pet to slot into your life.

'Right, looks like I'm going to the reservoirs,' I said to Jo. 'Everything going OK with training?'

Jo rolled her eyes. 'You know: the owls are still awful. But we'll get there.'

She walked with me and Monkey to the car and waved us off, before heading back to the paddocks.

'Lots of people to meet today,' I told Monkey, catching his eye in the rear-view mirror. 'Next up is Lisa – I think you're going to love her.'

The Tring reservoirs were one of my favourite spots to walk the dogs, and a regular haunt for Lisa too. The four man-made lakes had originally been built to serve the canal system, but now they were home to a wealth of wildlife, making them popular with anglers and birdwatchers alike. There was something peaceful about the vast expanses of water, around which wound pretty paths where you could hear little but the chirruping of birds and the gentle slap of fishing lines being cast. From the frosts of winter when the trees stood stark and bare to the glorious summer when the cow parsley grew abundantly and hummed with bees, the reservoirs were always a lovely place to stroll.

At the car park at Wilstone Reservoir I spotted Lisa's Land Rover, and pulled in next to it. I got Monkey out of the boot and settled myself at a picnic table to wait for Lisa to return, Monkey stretching out at my feet. I would have loved to give him a walk, but as he had not long eaten I wanted to wait for him to digest fully before he had any more exercise. Michelle's warning about bloat was still ringing in my ears.

I gazed out across the impossibly still water, grateful for the sun on my face. I hoped the good weather would hold – it certainly made training easier.

My thoughts were interrupted by a familiar silhouette rounding the corner: Lala, my Dalmatian. Behind her came the boxers, George and Ginelli, followed by Gypsy – still yapping away – and finally Lisa, with my pretty Yorkshire terrier Pickles trotting obediently at her ankles. I waved to Lisa and she waved back. Spotting Monkey by my side, she hurried to put the other dogs on their leads – good practice when you're approaching an animal you don't know.

'Hi!' she called out to me as she approached,

expertly juggling the five leads so that no one got tangled up. 'You got a new Fang, then?'

'Yep, this is Monkey,' I said. 'You're OK to let the others approach, I want to see how he is with new dogs.'

Lisa loosened the leads a little and Lala and Ginelli were the first over. Monkey was quivering with excitement, but maybe a little nervousness too. I kept a tight hold on his lead while Lala and Ginelli gave him a good sniff, which he happily returned, his desperation to play humming through him. As the other dogs came over to investigate him Monkey promptly threw himself on the ground in a gesture of submission, his great big paws waggling comically in the air. Lisa and I laughed to see tiny Pickles giving giant Monkey the once-over while he lay there, prostrate on the grass.

'Oh, isn't he gorgeous!' said Lisa, as Monkey scrambled to his feet again and bounced happily among his new friends. 'I've never seen a dog quite like him – but how can anyone have let him get so skinny?'

I smiled to see how enamoured she was with Monkey straight away, and took the leads from her so she could greet him properly. She held out her hand towards him and he gently licked it, looking up at her with those puppy-dog eyes.

'He's had a tough start in life, but I think he's got a heart of gold,' I told her.

Lisa sat down next to me and Monkey put his head in her lap. The other dogs quickly lost interest, with Pickles and Gypsy distracted by a manky old bottle they'd found which they decided to play tug of war with. But I could tell a special bond was forming between Lisa and Monkey as she tickled him behind the ears.

'Listen, Lisa, I've got my hands full with this lot,' I said, gesturing to my dogs. 'So I was wondering … How would you feel about Monkey coming to live with you? I'll have him for most of the day, of course, up at the studios, but it would be up to you to give him a proper home with all the TLC he deserves.'

Lisa looked up at me, her eyes shining. 'Are you serious? I can really take him home?'

I nodded. 'I wish I could have him myself, but you'd be doing me a massive favour if you did,' I said. 'He's big, and as you can see he's got a slight drooling problem, and I can tell you now he's pretty boisterous – but I reckon you can handle all that. And he really seems to be the most loving, sweet soul who just wants a bit of kindness. What do you think?'

Lisa's smile was so wide it looked like it would split her face in half. 'I would love to,' she said happily.

'Wonderful,' I beamed. 'Let's drop this lot home, then I'll come back to yours with you and we can get Monkey settled.'

As we loaded the dogs back into the cars, I felt a sudden pang that I was about to be parted from Monkey so soon after I had found him. I would still see him every day and I knew it was the right thing to do, but I couldn't help but feel I was going to miss him. How had I fallen in love with this daft dog so fast?

Chapter Twelve

Home or Away

On the way to Lisa's house – a couple of villages over, about a ten-minute drive from mine – we stopped at my favourite animal goods supplier so I could buy Monkey a big squashy bed, a supply of food, a selection of toys and of course some treats.

Lisa had recently moved in to a spacious place of her own with a long garden at the back, which I knew would be perfect for Monkey. He would be sharing it with her three cats.

'We'll have to introduce him to them carefully,'

I told her. 'If dogs haven't lived with cats before, the instinct to chase can be strong.'

Lisa grinned. 'They're the kind of cats that don't take any crap,' she said. 'I reckon they'll put him in his place pretty quickly.'

When we arrived at her house I stayed outside with Monkey while Lisa went inside to move anything breakable out of his reach. He was like a canine tornado and it just seemed sensible, for his sake and hers, to make sure there was nothing in his path. As we waited, I threw a ball for Monkey in the garden, which he tore after with infectious enthusiasm, even though he hadn't quite got the hang of bringing it back. He would pick it up, drop it again, then hurl himself back towards me for a cuddle. I still had no idea if we'd be able to use him in the film, but somehow his vibrant nature had driven all the stress about Fang from my mind.

'Ready!' called Lisa from the back door. She ushered Monkey inside and he was full of beans, racing round the downstairs and sniffing every inch of his new home. As he got himself acquainted with the new sights and smells, we set up Monkey's bed, lined with a fleecy tartan blanket, in a cosy corner of Lisa's kitchen where he would have plenty of space to sprawl out. I jotted down a feeding schedule and told her to take it easy with the exercise to begin with.

'He seems like he has a lot of energy but he's burning through calories he doesn't have,' I said. 'We've got to get some weight on him, so just short, gentle walks for the time being.'

I could tell Lisa was going to provide a lovely haven for Monkey, and that he'd be very happy with her. Finally, there was nothing left to do but say goodbye.

'All right then, I'll leave you to it!' I said, trying to keep it breezy. The plan was that Lisa would bring Monkey with her when she came for my dogs every morning, and I would take him to the studios with me. I wanted him to get used to the routine of being on set, and to introduce him to training as soon as possible at the facility up there. If he wasn't going to take to it I needed to know pretty soon, because there was so little time left to find an alternative dog. And if he was, he had a lot to learn – and I would have a packed schedule getting him ready.

'See you tomorrow, big man,' I said, giving him a final cuddle, and wiping trails of slobber from my jeans. Working with Monkey, I was certainly going to get through a lot of clothes.

Lisa waved me off from the doorstep, and I could see the eagerness in her eyes. I knew how she felt – when you love animals, having responsibility for a new one is about as exciting as it gets.

There was a lot about Lisa that reminded me of myself when I was first starting out. I was nineteen when my dream of being a movie animal trainer was born. At the time, I was dating a guy whose dad worked on low-budget indie films, and he was shooting one that required a dog.

He asked if I might be able to borrow one from the grooming parlour where I worked and bring it along to the set to shoot some scenes. I was thrilled – after all, I was obsessed with teaching tricks to Sally, the rescue Border collie cross my parents had got me when I was eleven. However, the film called for a spaniel, so I borrowed one named Ben and taught him the commands he'd need. We spent a brilliant, magical day on set and I knew there and then I wanted to train movie animals for a living.

Like Lisa, I'd started breaking my way into the business by doing grooming, exercise and basic care for various companies before setting out on my own as a trainer. I wanted to do things a little differently, using rescue animals wherever I could and putting the welfare of the animals at the centre of everything I did. I was just starting to make a name for myself when Gary Gero hired me – and the rest is history.

My memories were interrupted by my mobile

phone ringing. I answered it just as I was getting into the car – it was Glenn.

'Hi babe!' he greeted me. 'How are you getting on? Successful day?'

'Very!' I said. 'I've got a lot to tell you about – I've got a new dog! But don't worry, this one isn't living with me.' Glenn had valiantly learned to love my furry brood, but he was always joking that if it got any bigger there wouldn't be room for him on the sofa.

'That's great,' he said. 'Why don't you tell me over dinner at my place? I've got a really early start tomorrow so would be great if we could stay at mine tonight.'

I paused. While I didn't want to be unreasonable, I really wanted to go back to my cottage that evening. Having been on the road all day I had hardly seen my animals, so was looking forward to some quality time with them. I wanted to do a little bit of refresher training with Pickles, who was still picking up lots of work in adverts and films. But I didn't want Glenn to think he was less important to me either.

As usual, Glenn could sense my hesitation. 'Come on, Jules,' he said. 'You know I don't ask very often. It sometimes feels like your life always take precedence over mine. I'm just asking for a little flexibility.'

Now that we were spending almost every night together, Glenn and I were having this disagreement every few weeks. I knew it was difficult for him, splitting his life between two places and hardly ever being at home for longer than a few hours. It wasn't fair that he always had to come to mine, but I simply had to put my animals first. He knew that about me when we got together, and to be fair to him he had always respected it. But it was getting tricky in situations like this.

'Glenn, I'd love to, but I need to be at home tonight,' I said. 'I'm really sorry. If you feel like you can't come over that's fine, I understand.'

He sighed. 'Feels like we keep going round in

circles on this one, doesn't it? Listen, let's just leave tonight. Maybe we should take a little break anyway. We'll figure something out when we're both less busy.'

'OK, if that's what you want,' I said, working hard not to sound too upset. I had really been looking forward to telling him all about Monkey. 'I love you,' I added, trying not to sound like I was pleading for him to say it back.

'Love you too,' said Glenn gruffly, and rang off. I groaned, and started the engine.

This is why I'd been single for so long: having a relationship while you were already devoted to an entire family of dependent, furry creatures who didn't allow for much spontaneity in your life wasn't exactly easy. Glenn had been so understanding with me for so long, but was his patience running out? I couldn't bear the thought of losing him – but what could I do?

Chapter Thirteen

Leavesden Nothing to Chance

When I woke the next morning I rolled over to Glenn's side of the bed, in my half-sleep expecting to find his warm body there. Finding it cold and empty, the previous night's argument came flooding back to me, putting paid to any hope of any further peaceful dozing.

Pickles, who could always sense when something was wrong, crawled up from the end of the bed where she had been curled and snuggled into my chest. I breathed in her warm doggy scent as I hugged her close. 'You'll never leave me will you, treasure?' I said. She wriggled and licked my cheek. I felt a surge of gratitude that, no matter what was going on in my life, I could always rely on the steady and unwavering love of my canine and feline companions.

As I took the dogs for their morning walk I tried to put thoughts of my personal life to the back of my mind, because today was important; it was Monkey's first proper day at the studios. I hoped to use it to acclimatise him to the surroundings which would hopefully be his second home for the coming months. I also wanted to see how he reacted around different people and scenarios, to check if he had any triggers or behavioural issues that would need working on. I would use the first fortnight just to build a relationship with him and assess whether he was going to be right for the film, before I started a full-on training regime.

So far I knew he was quite boisterous, which I hoped could be channelled into him learning tricks and commands. It was a fine balance, though, and if he was just too naughty and head-strong it might be too much of a challenge to get him ready in time. Although he was a sweetie, he barked a lot and had absolutely no control on the lead, so we had a long way to go before he could be trusted on a set.

I wondered if I was mad, taking a chance on Monkey with so little time before *The Goblet of Fire* started filming. Maybe I should keep looking to see if I could find a lease dog who might at least know the basics? But then there was just something about Monkey that told me it was worth persevering. I resolved to see how today went before I rushed into any decisions.

Back at the cottage, my animals had just fin-ished off their breakfast when Lisa arrived. This morning there was more of a commotion than usual because she had Monkey with her. Through the open window I could hear her chatting away to him as she got him out of her car, and stopped to watch them make their way up the garden path. They made a funny pair, her so petite and him so big and lanky.

'Hi loves!' I called, opening the door. 'How did you get on last night?'

Lisa was still smiling, which was good news. 'Really well,' she said brightly. 'He pretty much crashed after you left – too much excitement for one day. But he woke up when I went up to bed and then he just wouldn't stop crying. He has some separation anxiety, I think. In the end I just moved his bed into my room and that seemed to do the trick.'

I was making a fuss of Monkey, who was beside himself to see me again. 'He's clearly a very loving dog,' I said. 'I wonder what happened to him in his past life. Maybe he was left on his own too much and it's made him a bit anxious.'

Lisa nodded. 'I reckon so too. Every time he

goes out into the garden I have to go with him because he can't bear it if I shut the kitchen door. I think he thinks I'm going to leave him there.'

'It's up to us to make sure he knows no one is going to abandon him again,' I said. 'Training will help. Has he been eating all right?'

'Yes, I gave him small meals like you said but he licked the bowl clean on each,' said Lisa. 'He's a hungry boy, that's for sure.'

I left Lisa to bid her farewells to Monkey while I packed Max and Crackerjack into their travelling crates. I was taking them to the studios too as we had some cat training scheduled.

Monkey hopped happily enough into the back of the Shogun and then we were off, waving goodbye to Lisa and the other dogs.

It wasn't far to Leavesden from Long Marston – it was part of the reason why I had chosen the village when I had taken the plunge and moved out of London last year. Monkey was a much better passenger than he had been the previous day, with only about ten minutes of barking before he settled down to snooze. The sound of his heavy snores filling the car made me giggle.

By 9.30 a.m. I was pulling into my usual spot in the studio car park. I usually went up to the main set before I headed down to the training ground so I could grab a bacon roll and a coffee from the canteen. Food here was always delicious and plentiful.

Ever since the very first *Potter* film started shooting in 2000, Leavesden had become the closest thing to an office to me. It really was a place like no other. Warner Bros had chosen it as the *Potter* HQ, rather than Britain's more famous studios, Pinewood and Shepperton, because of the space and potential it offered.

The complex had previously been home to Rolls-Royce, who used it to build aeroplane engines as part of the war effort. The working factory closed in the eighties, leaving a vast half a million square feet of space, plus eighty acres of surrounding land. The James Bond movie *GoldenEye* was the first to use it as a studio, followed by films including *Sleepy Hollow* and *Star Wars: The Phantom Menace*. As a film fan, I always got a bit of a thrill from the history of the place.

Since it had become the home of *Harry Potter*, Leavesden had transformed into a sort of village where a huge technical crew worked round the clock to bring the magic of J. K. Rowling's best-selling books to life. The best in the business had semi-permanent bases where they devoted themselves to designing, creating and perfecting the details that would make the wizarding world so rich on screen, from the wands to the magical creatures to the amazing special effects. As animal trainers we were just a small cog in the vast machine, but I felt immensely proud to be working alongside such talented and creative people on a daily basis.

I spotted my friend Gordon, who worked in

props, pulling up in his car, and gave him a wave as I unloaded Monkey. One of the nicest things about the *Potter* franchise was that many of us had been working on it for four years now, so we had got to know each other well.

'Hi Jules!' Gordon greeted me. He was dressed in jeans and a checked shirt, his dark hair ruffled, a file full of notes under his arm. 'That's not Hugo is it? Is it a new dog I spy?'

'Well spotted!' I answered warmly. 'This is my new Fang: his name is Monkey. Don't worry, he's going to be a bit fatter by the time we get him on screen!'

Gordon was a dog lover and I knew he was dying to say hello. 'I'm actually trying to see how he reacts in different situations today, so do please come and stroke him.' So far, I'd only introduced Monkey to two women, and I wanted to see if he was as relaxed around men. Some dogs, especially those who have been abused, can react in unexpected ways to different genders.

Gordon approached slowly as I had taught him to do, holding out his hand to Monkey so he could see he was no threat, before giving him a pat.

I held my breath, my knuckles white as they gripped Monkey's lead. Was I imagining it, or was Monkey more tense than he had been meeting Jo and Lisa?

Monkey took a step back, and for a moment I worried that he was about to growl. Plenty of the Neapolitan mastiffs I had encountered before had been mistrustful of new people and aggressive in this sort of situation.

But then Monkey collapsed to the floor, rolling on his back in submission. Gordon chuckled and rubbed his belly, which made Monkey shiver with delight. I was relieved to see he didn't seem to mind who was making a fuss of him, as long as someone was.

'He's a beautiful boy,' said Gordon. 'I hope he settles in well.'

We wished each other a good day and Gordon headed towards the prop department, which was housed in the sprawling network of cabins inside one of the huge hangars. I got my breakfast to take away, pleased by how Monkey waited patiently at my side while the caterers popped it into a box for me.

I put Monkey back into the car and drove the short distance to our training ground, on the edge of the studio complex. Monkey had proved himself remarkably good natured so far, but it was still early days. I had no idea how he would take to training – did he have it in him to be my Fang?

Chapter Fourteen

Learning Curve

At the training ground, there were plenty more people for Monkey to meet. He took it all in his stride, lapping up the attention he was getting.

We had a busy schedule that day, doing more training with the owls but also working on scenes with the cats. Crackerjack, who played Crookshanks, didn't have anything particularly challenging to learn but I wanted to go over the basics, like going to a mark and sitting still on an actor's lap, before he was called on set. And I wanted to start teaching Max how to leap from the ground onto a shoulder, which was something he would be required to do with the actor David Bradley, who played Hogwarts caretaker Argus Filch.

As for Monkey, I just wanted him to get used to being around the other trainers and the routine of the training ground. I wouldn't be starting his training in earnest until he was back to full health, but I did want to introduce him to some short fifteen-minute sessions to get him used to learning with me. The sooner I was confident he would take basic commands like heel and sit, the sooner I would feel comfortable carefully introducing him to children. At the moment he was a bit too wild and headstrong to take the risk.

While I worked with the cats, I put Monkey in the dog run we had constructed, and Caroline, one of our animal maintenance team, would keep him company. I didn't want to shut him in on his own until he was over the worst of his separation anxiety, so asked Caroline to make sure she was always within sight. 'No problem,' she grinned. 'Won't be a chore keeping this one occupied!'

There was an indoor area at one end, with a comfy bed and lots of toys, and a grassy run where he could play. It seemed to meet with Monkey's approval; he was perfectly happy pottering around or having a snooze while I worked, taking frequent breaks so I could throw a ball for him or take him for a quick stroll around the studios. I wanted to make sure he knew he could rely on me as someone who would always come back to him and who would make his day fun. To be honest, it was hard to tear myself away from him – there was something about him that just made me smile.

After lunch – shepherd's pie and peas: delicious – I decided it was time for the first training session. I clipped on my bait belt – a sort of pouch I wear while training, with a pocket full of tasty treats to reward the animals when they get something right. I led Monkey up into one of the paddocks, which was out of sight of where the other trainers were working with their animals, so that there wouldn't be any distractions.

'Right, Monkey,' I said. 'It's school time – I need you to concentrate.'

I reached into the bait belt for a bit of sausage, and before I even had his name out of my mouth Monkey was jumping up to snatch it from my hand. I quickly whipped it back into the pocket, and Monkey fell back in disappointment, unable to work out where it had gone. I couldn't have him stealing treats – he needed to learn they came as a reward.

'Let's try again,' I said. I took a step away from him, then called the command. 'Come!'

Instinctively, Monkey came straight to me, and I gave him the treat and lots of fuss. 'Well done!'

Working with animals who don't even know simple commands like come and sit can be slow progress – but so rewarding. I could see Monkey warming to the task as I walked away from him and called him to me. The next step would be getting him to wait before I called him, but for now I could see him start to associate the command with getting a treat if he came to me. I couldn't help but smile as he lumbered towards me, all puppyish limbs and floppy rolls of skin. He was like a dog from a cartoon.

After fifteen minutes, it was time to stop – although I could sense Monkey's disappointment when he realised the bait belt was going away. 'Don't worry, we'll do some more later,' I said, patting his velvety head.

It had only been a short lesson, but already I could tell Monkey had what it took to be a good pupil. He seemed to enjoy himself and responded quickly. There was a lot of work to do, but my confidence that he was the right dog for the job was growing.

My usual approach when starting with a new animal was to spend the first couple of weeks doing these short sessions, working on the basics. With Monkey, we'd build up to doing about six sessions a day as he got stronger. After a few weeks we would move on to one of the most important things any movie animal can learn: going to a mark. A mark is a small wooden block which we train the animal to put their paws on, and allows us to move them around a scene as the director requires.

Once he'd nailed that, I would move on to teaching Monkey the specific behaviours he'd need for the film. By then we would be doing longer sessions of thirty minutes, about four times a day. He'd have to learn how to bark on command, how to look scared, how to lower his head and how to mirror his on-screen owner, Robbie Coltrane, who played Hagrid. I would teach him how to cover his face with his paws and how to move backwards, as well as crawl on his belly and jump over an obstacle.

Harry Potter productions typically shot way more

footage than they needed, so it was always better to have the animals over prepared, because you never knew what they would be called on to do.

Whatever I did, though, I made sure training sessions were fun and stimulating for the animals. It's why I keep them so short, even if it seems like the animal could easily keep working for longer. I never want to push them towards a point where they are no longer engaged and enjoying it, because training shouldn't be a chore. Once it becomes a battle of wills, as a trainer you are only ever going to lose. So it was far better to leave Monkey wanting more than to push him to his limit, especially when he was still so skinny. Working with him all day and seeing how bony he was, I felt almost sick about it. It broke my heart to think his former owners had starved him so badly. Even though I had a plan to get the weight back on him, it was shocking to see.

Towards the end of the day, I was sitting on the grass with Monkey lying beside me, enjoying the last of the afternoon sun. We'd just completed a second training session and he was worn out. Mental exercise can be just as taxing as physical for some dogs.

I checked my phone for maybe the fiftieth time that day, and blinked back my disappointment when I saw there was still no text from Glenn. He really was taking a break from us then.

Monkey had been such a welcome distraction from the drama in my personal life throughout the day, but now that I'd stopped I could feel the tears welling in my eyes. I rubbed them furiously away, annoyed with myself that I had got so upset. As if he could sense something was wrong, Monkey shifted upright and stared at me, his dark brown eyes full of gentleness. Shuffling closer, he gave my hand a tentative lick then plopped his head into my lap. I stroked the soft folds of his face gratefully – there's nothing like a hug to make you feel better, and this was definitely Monkey's version of a good cuddle.

Jo came to join us, two mugs in her hands, flop-ping down on the grass next to me. She handed me one of the steaming teas. 'What's up, then, Jules?' she said. 'You've been very quiet today.'

I sighed and took a sip of tea. I'd been hoping that the other trainers would assume that I was spending more time on my own because I was devoting myself to Monkey, but I should have known better than to think I could fool Jo. She always knew when something was wrong.

'It's Glenn,' I said quietly. 'We had a bit of a fall-ing out last night. It feels like it's getting harder and harder for us to fit our lives round each other.'

Jo took a big gulp of tea. 'Maybe you need to stop seeing it as two separate lives,' she said. 'You love Glenn, right? And anyone who's seen you together knows he's absolutely crazy about you too. So why not share your life rather than keep trying to compromise?' She shrugged like it was the simplest thing in the world.

'You know, for an animal trainer you're not

bad on humans either,' I told her. She laughed, putting her arm round my shoulders.

'You two will figure it out,' she said.

'I hope that's true. I hate feeling like this.'

Monkey decided now was the time to rouse himself again, and he tried to squeeze himself between the two of us, so determined he was to join in the embrace. We both fell about laughing as he clambered all over us, slobber, paws and spilt tea going everywhere.

'See, Monkey knows that if you love someone, just show them!' screamed Jo as he wriggled his bony bottom on my lap and shoved his head onto her shoulder.

I could hardly catch my breath from laughing – but it had given me an idea.

Chapter Fifteen

Moving Forwards

I headed home early: Monkey was exhausted, and I wanted to get him back to Lisa. Plus, it would give me time to take my dogs for an evening stroll through the dappled shade of the woods before Glenn finished work.

On the way back to the cottage, we passed by his barn conversion. I nipped up the driveway – the absence of his silver sports car telling me he still wasn't home – and popped the note I'd scribbled down earlier through the letterbox.

'We need to talk. I'll be waiting in the pub at 8 – I hope you'll join me. J.'

Once it was posted, there was no going back. I hurried home and made the animals their dinner, then jumped in the shower.

Ten minutes later I was towelling my long blond hair dry. Glenn was used to seeing me in jeans and old sweaters covered in dog hair, but I wanted tonight to be more special. I rooted in the back of my wardrobe until I found a faithful little black dress, which I slipped on with a pair of heeled ankle boots. I carefully slicked my lashes with mascara and painted my lips a pretty pink. Looking in the mirror, I wasn't displeased with the effect.

'OK, wish me luck!' I told my assembled heap of doggy pals, who looked up at me sleepily from the sofa. Comfy and companionable, I knew they'd be OK on their own for a couple of hours.

The Queen's Head was just a short walk from the cottage, which was just as well because I was never very good at walking in heels. It was a charming double-fronted building in the centre of the village, painted white and supposedly over five hundred years old.

Inside it was cosy and oak beamed, and always filled with the cheery laughter of the locals who had made it a community hub. It was also a special place for Glenn and me – it was where we had met, and where our friendship had blossomed before we realised that we both wanted something more.

I was ten minutes early, and I could feel the butterflies in my stomach. Would he come? Or was he still annoyed? Maybe he would think it weird that I had sent the note rather than called or texted. But I needed to have this conversation in person, and I didn't want to get into any back and forth beforehand.

As I waited, I ordered a red wine for me and a Guinness for him. I really had to hope he wasn't going to stand me up now, or I'd look pretty silly sitting there with two drinks. I smoothed down my dress nervously and checked my phone again: nothing.

The low pub door swung open and I jumped, just as I had every time anyone had come in since I'd arrived. This time, though, it was Glenn. His face looked pale and drawn, and he pushed his hand distractedly through his mousy hair as he scanned the pub looking for me. I waved, and it was as if the air was knocked out of him. He hurried over.

'Jules. You don't have to do this,' he said, his voice low and urgent, his hands reaching across the table for mine. 'Look, I'm so sorry. I've been an idiot. Let's just forget about last night just – don't.' He clenched his eyes shut, and when they opened again I could see they were filled with pain and confusion.

'Don't what?' I said, baffled myself. 'What do you think I'm going to do?'

'You're breaking up with me, aren't you?' Glenn replied, and his voice was full of sorrow.

'Glenn! Of course I'm not. I – I love you, I brought you here because—'

'"We need to talk" can only mean one thing—'

'—I wanted to apologise. I never want you to feel like you are second best.'

Glenn was still gripping my hands, and his eyes searched my face for clues. 'You don't make me feel like that,' he sighed. 'I was being selfish last night. I was just tired. But I shouldn't have taken it out on you.'

Gently, I released his hands, and reached into my bag. 'It's OK,' I told him. 'I understand. It's hard, living between two places. Which is why I hoped – that maybe you'll consider – moving in with me.'

I placed the spare key to my cottage on the table between us. There was a silence while Glenn stared at it. I held my breath, feeling a heady jumble of emotions course through me as I waited on tenterhooks for what he would say.

Glenn let out his breath in a low whistle.

He picked the key up, like he'd never seen one before. Then he caught my eye and his whole face cracked into a magnificent smile.

'You're too good for me, Jules,' he said. 'Of course I will!'

We were on our feet then, holding each other close like we never wanted to let go. I felt all the tension and stress of the last twenty-four hours lifting off me like a cloud.

'Well, this is pretty exciting,' said Glenn when we finally let go, and clinked our glasses together in celebration. 'Roomies at last!'

We spent the next couple of hours in a blur of animated chatter, discussing what Glenn would bring and where he would put it. He said he thought he'd hold on to the barn and maybe rent it out, but he couldn't wait to have all his stuff in one place. We joked about setting up a rota for chores and what secret habits we might discover in each other. I was used to my own space, and had fiercely guarded it for a long time. But the idea of Glenn moving in just felt so right, and I was too thrilled to feel nervous.

We wandered back through the chilly night air arm in arm, finally falling silent as we both peacefully contemplated our new future stretching out in front of us. When we reached the front door, Glenn swept me into his arms and pulled his new key from his pocket with a flourish.

'Home sweet home!' he joked, as I giggled. But he was right – that night, knowing Glenn was here for good, the cottage never felt more like home.

Chapter Sixteen

Learning Lines

Glenn moved his stuff in the very next day. Chaotic boxes of records, clothes and old trainers had seamlessly blended with my own things before I knew it. The dogs, who had always competed for Glenn's attention, were delighted to have him around full time. I caught him one morning chatting away to Pickles, curled in his lap, as he ate his toast. I smiled to myself; when we first met, and he was wary of even patting her because of his allergies, this would have been unthinkable.

Asking him to move in turned out to be one of the best decisions I've ever made. I loved the familiarity of knowing he'd always be there, and the weekends felt long and luxurious rather than an asset to be negotiated over. It was weird, considering he'd only lived a ten-minute walk away before, how big a difference it made.

Meanwhile, Monkey was going from strength to strength. He had adapted well to having two mums – me in the day and Lisa in the evening. Each time the handover seemed to come as a glorious surprise to him, as if he had forgotten what would be in store, and he would be beside himself with excitement when he jumped out of Lisa's car and found himself at my cottage. Likewise, when I brought him home in the evening and he caught sight of Lisa, he'd lose it all over again. Dogs love routine and Monkey had taken to his with aplomb – which in turn had sorted out his separation anxiety. He no longer cried, for instance, when Lisa went up to bed and left him downstairs. Life for him was now one long parade of delights to be savoured and enjoyed, and I couldn't help but catch a little of his infectious enthusiasm.

Up at the studios, Monkey and I were working on sit, stay and recall, with him coming back to me from further and further away. It was a step up from what I had done with him on the very first day, but I couldn't say it was completely smooth progress. At the training ground we worked on it little and often and he always came, eagerly looking for a treat. But when I took him for longer walks around the studio complex he would often get distracted – the smell of a rabbit, or the sight of someone wheeling a trolley full of supplies in the distance – and then my commands would fall on deaf ears. I had taken to walking him on a long lead so I could grab the tail end of it if he was about to run off, and I was trying to get him used to coming to a whistle too. Lisa was reinforcing the training I did with him on their evening walks, and I was hopeful he'd get the hang of it soon – he was already showing some improvement, which was good because there wasn't much time left to work on this sort of basic training. I was getting a little nervous. One of the assistant directors was due down at the training ground any day now and would want to see how we were getting on with all the animals, including Fang. Monkey ignoring something as simple as his own name wouldn't be very impressive.

On the other hand, I had always said that my priority was getting him well, and in that department at least we were making good progress.

Lisa and I were both working hard at keeping the balance between feeding Monkey enough that he'd put on weight but not so much that it would upset his stomach. It was heartening to see that our dedication was paying off. Every day Monkey looked less painfully skinny, and some gentle exercise was starting to build up his wasted muscles. I realised I was no longer wincing when I looked at him – he was still slim, but in a puppyish way rather than because he was severely malnourished.

When I took him back to Michelle for a weigh-in, she hadn't even put him on the scales before she had declared him a 'chunky Monkey'. There was much hilarity as we tried to wrestle him onto the scales, while he was far more intent on trying to roll over or lick Michelle's face. When we did finally manage to get him to stand still, the results were clear – he'd increased his body-weight by 20 per cent and was well on his way to his target weight of 60kg.

'That's brilliant news!' Lisa exclaimed when I dropped Monkey back at hers and filled her in on what had happened. 'We're getting there, aren't we?'

'We certainly are,' I smiled. 'Thank you, Lisa, for all the love and care you've given him – I couldn't have done it without you.'

'Oh, don't be silly,' she said, waving my words away. 'It's been such a privilege having him in my life. And knowing he's going to be in *Harry Potter* too! You reckon he's going to be ready soon?'

It was a question I'd been turning over in my head on the drive back from the vet's. I'd been wary about pushing Monkey too hard or too fast because I wanted to focus on his health. But now he'd put some weight on and seemed so full of energy, there was no reason not to ramp up his training. Filming had already started, and Monkey's scenes were scheduled for about a month and a half's time. The clock was ticking.

'Yes, I'm going to start teaching him some of the specific tricks this week,' I said. 'And I still need to introduce him to some of the kids. I'm not really worried about it, but it needs to be done – if he's funny around them I can't risk having him act alongside them.'

'I reckon he'll be great,' said Lisa, glancing over to where Monkey was sprawled on a fluffy rug in the middle of the living room. 'Although I guess I'm biased . . .'

I adored Monkey too, but there were still niggling worries at the back of my mind. Would I be able to calm him down enough to take on set? Could I trust him not to be naughty, run off or chew props to pieces? The sight of the various mangled remains of toys around Lisa's living room told me he had an appetite for destruction.

As if he knew we were talking about him, Monkey opened one eye. When he saw we were watching him, he happily bustled over and put his head in my lap, looking up at me with pure devotion. Somehow I felt instantly calmer. This dog would do anything for me; I just needed to put my faith in him. He wouldn't let me down – would he?

Chapter Seventeen

School Days

Monkey wasn't exactly naughty, but he was a teenager in dog years, and that meant he was constantly pushing his boundaries. All dogs of his age could be a little challenging, especially if they haven't been trained or socialised well as puppies. Monkey was still so young when he had been abandoned, and it was as if he wanted to make up for it now. I loved how energetic, playful and curious he was – it meant he relished our training sessions as much as I did.

I truly believe that training can enrich an animal's life in vital ways. It provides mental as well as physical stimulation, and dogs love keeping their minds busy. It is also a great way to build a relationship between you and your animal. When you set up training to help your dog succeed, you become a proper team.

Training should always be reward based: there's no point in yelling at a dog if, for example, they jump up. For a dog, this kind of attention is better than no attention at all, so they may end up doing it more. Monkey tried jumping up at me at few times but when I steadfastly ignored him – quite difficult when you have an enormous mastiff practically at eye level! – he sat back down again. That's when I would give him lots of fuss, and he quickly learned that jumping up wasn't worth it.

Little adjustments like this meant that Monkey was quickly becoming a more manageable dog, while retaining that irresistible personality of his. But just getting better behaved wasn't going to be enough. I needed to start teaching him the specific things he needed for the film.

With his recall improving, I moved on to teaching him to walk to heel. Monkey was a big, strong dog and taking him for even a very short walk on the lead was a proper workout because he was always dragging ahead. As Fang, he would have to walk obediently at Hagrid's side, so it was a really important thing for him to master.

I started off by having him on a short lead, a treat in one hand. I gave the command 'heel' and slowly walked forward a few paces. Transfixed by the treat, Monkey stuck by my side – but only managed a couple of steps before he heard one of the cats yowling in the distance and started ploughing towards the edge of the paddock.

'No, let's try again,' I told him. The treat in my hand, I gave him the command again. This time, we managed the length of the paddock without him trying to pull, and I rewarded him every few paces with a scrap of chicken and lots of praise. 'Clever boy!'

Over the following week, we practised heel walking over and over. We progressed from the short lead to a longer one, which I let trail behind Monkey on the ground, so I could step on it to stop him running off if he lost his focus. It seemed like no time before we were doing it with no lead at all. As luck would have it, Jane, the assistant director, arrived for her inspection on the first day Monkey really nailed walking to heel.

'So this is our new Fang!' I told her, walking up and down with Monkey obediently trotting beside me so she could see him in motion. 'He's still got a few things to learn but we're getting there.'

'He looks good,' she smiled. 'Looking forward to seeing him on set.'

By now I had been working with Monkey for a month, and filming started in just a fortnight's time. Monkey's scenes weren't scheduled for several weeks but the pressure was definitely on. As well as heel, he had got the hang of sit, stay, lie down and come (when he felt like it). Now he was starting to learn how to go to a mark – although he still quite often picked up the wooden block and ran around with it like it was a toy. We needed to work on that one, and whenever I saw him delightedly chewing another wooden block I would feel a familiar wash of nervousness. He absolutely couldn't do that on set – but, I reassured myself, he was still learning.

The following Monday, Monkey and I were back at the studios, and it was the first of his longer, thirty-minute training sessions. Today, however, I wanted to teach him how to bark on cue. Monkey loved the sound of his own voice so I hoped this wouldn't be too tricky for him. The challenge was going to be getting him to bark when I wanted him to, rather than when he felt like it.

I knew that with Monkey the best way to teach

him anything was to make it a fun game. Luckily, my training method for barking lends itself to this. I led him into our usual paddock, then I let myself out, shutting the gate carefully behind me. Monkey trotted straight to it and poked his head through, curious to see what would happen next.

All of a sudden, I started to run away, waving my arms around like a madwoman and making lots of noise. You can't be self-conscious in this job!

With all the commotion, Monkey started barking at me. It was his way of saying 'Let me out! I want to join in!' And it was exactly what I wanted. As he barked I repeated the command I would use – 'Speak!' – and threw him the treat.

Within seconds I was back with him, giving him lots of love. 'Good boy!' I could tell he was excited now, and keen to go again.

This time, when I shut him in the paddock he galloped over and put his paws on the bars of the gate. I didn't run away in such a crazy way, just stepped backwards and gave the command: 'Speak!'

Monkey barked and barked, his big booming voice ringing out around the paddock. I was so pleased – he was picking it up fast, and really enjoying it.

We practised a few more times, Monkey getting more and more hyper as he warmed to the game. After he nailed it again and again with the gate, I decided to join him in the paddock and simply give the command. He didn't quite get it: at first, when I said 'speak' he'd just run to the gate, thinking that was what I wanted.

I kept my patience and with plenty of repetition he figured it out. 'Speak!' I'd say, and he'd respond with that amazing bark, as rich and velvety as his coat had become.

I was so absorbed in our noisy work that I hadn't noticed an audience had assembled behind me. So I got quite a shock when I heard someone call my name. I spun round, to find three teenagers with their feet resting on the bottom rail of the fence.

'Hi Julie! Is this your new dog? Can we say hello?'

Chapter Eighteen

Child's Play

I took in the smiling, eager faces of Emma Watson, who played Hermione Granger, Matthew Lewis, who played Neville Longbottom, and Devon Murray, who played Seamus Finnigan. They were dressed casually – the boys in shorts and T-shirts, Emma in a denim dress – clearly making the most of the warm May weather.

Automatically, I grabbed hold of Monkey's

collar, although he hadn't made a move towards the kids, and clipped him on to the lead that was looped around my shoulder.

It wasn't that I wasn't pleased to see them – after four years working alongside these youngsters they were like family – but they had taken me a little by surprise. In the schedule I had laid out, I had planned to work with Monkey on his obedience for at least another two weeks before I introduced him to any children, to make sure he was as calm and controlled around them as possible. But I supposed Monkey's barks carrying on the breeze had probably caught their attention and brought them hurrying down to see what was going on.

'Hi guys! How lovely to see you,' I greeted them, and meant it. I could still see these three as wide-eyed eleven-year-olds, on set for the first time; they had seemed like such little children. It was hard to believe they had grown into the sophisticated teenagers in front of me now. One minute they're playing Pokémon in their down-time, and then what seems like the next minute they're talking about their boyfriend or girlfriend. It's a cliché, but they really do grow up so fast!

This year I knew many of the cast members were studying hard for their GCSEs, fitting a tough educational schedule around filming. No wonder they wanted to escape when they could, and coming to check out the newest canine cast member was the perfect excuse.

'He's a new one, isn't he?' asked Matthew, who seemed to get taller every time I saw him, nodding at Monkey. He was a real animal lover, and he could see this wasn't Hugo, despite their similarities.

'Yes, this is Monkey,' I said. 'He's a lovely friendly boy, but I haven't introduced him to any teenagers yet. I'm sure he'll be very gentle, but just come in carefully and don't crowd him all at once.'

Following my instructions to the letter, the

trio unlatched the gate and approached slowly. Monkey strained at his lead, whimpering in a kind of overwhelmed excitement. Matthew was the first to reach his hand out towards him, and as soon as he did Monkey collapsed onto his back, legs waving in the air, his typical greeting for people he loved.

Emma, Matthew and Devon giggled, and soon they were all giving him lots of pats and strokes. Monkey was absolutely in his element. He wriggled to his feet and went from one to the other demanding attention, then gave a joyful shake, splattering them all with drool.

Luckily, none of them minded. They all laughed hysterically. 'New dog, same drool problem!' joked Devon.

'We're just about done here and I'm about to take him for a walk, actually,' I told them, once we had stopped laughing. 'Do you want to join me, and you can tell me what you've been up to?'

They didn't need asking twice, and we all set

off along the grassy paths that ran around the perimeter of the studio complex. I always used these walks to work on Monkey's recall, which was pretty perfect now, using a whistle as an extra tool to reinforce the vocal command. But today he didn't need much reinforcement – he was enjoying bouncing around the kids too much to stray.

As we wandered across the sun-drenched fields, the teenagers chatted away to me about the scenes they'd been shooting, and the amazing sets they had seen being assembled up at the main site. This *Potter* film was about Harry, played by Daniel Radcliffe, competing in the Triwizard Tournament, which involved lots of different challenges, including him fighting a dragon and diving into the Great Lake at Hogwarts to rescue his friend Ron, played by Rupert Grint.

'Dan's been filming underwater in this big tank for days,' Emma told me, tucking her thick brown hair behind her ears. 'They can only film, like, a minute of footage at a time. So it's taking ages, but it's going to look so cool when it's done. I've got to do some too next week, so I'm practising my swimming.'

I loved to hear them talk like this, full of enthusiasm about the film project. They worked hard but the atmosphere on set was always one of encouragement, with the welfare of the young actors always a priority. We were on our third director now – Chris Columbus had done the first two films, followed by Alfonso Cuarón and now Mike Newell. But it was a returning cast and many of the crew members had also stayed with the production, so it was a very well-established community who had got to know each other and built up an impressive amount of trust.

'Sounds fab,' I told Emma. 'They've always got a new challenge for you up their sleeve, haven't they?'

The boys were a little ahead of us, and Matthew had spotted a tennis ball in the undergrowth – I reckoned it was probably one of Monkey's, which he must have lost out here a few days ago. Matthew picked it up and threw it for Monkey, who tore after it excitedly.

The ball bounced at a funny angle on a hillock, causing Monkey to have to rapidly change direction, his legs splaying out all over the place like spaghetti. I realised what was going to happen before it did. The ball was shooting towards a tree, which Monkey was now running towards at full pelt. And the trouble with Monkey was – well, he didn't really have a brake.

'Careful, Monkey!' I called, but it was too late: unable to stop himself in time, Monkey barged head-first into the tree. He bounced off it like he was made of rubber, seeming to hardly feel the impact, and immediately started spinning round looking for the ball. The kids were in hysterics again, and so was I – this big, clumsy oaf of a dog just had a knack for making you laugh.

I ran over to Monkey to check he was all right,

running my hands over him to make sure. But there seemed to be no harm done. Now he was running in crazy circles, so thrilled to be out for a walk with his new friends.

I couldn't believe I had been nervous about introducing him to the younger cast members. Well, it's always good to be cautious, especially because I knew Neapolitan mastiffs could be difficult dogs. But Monkey clearly loved being with kids more than anything. Which was just as well, seeing as there would be loads of them on set – not just the main cast, but all the extras too.

By the time we had completed a loop and arrived back at the animal training HQ, I could tell the three of them were reluctant to say goodbye. 'Got to go and do my maths homework,' said Devon grumpily, scuffing a stone with his toe.

'Well, you know where we are – Monkey will be very pleased to see you next time you get a break,' I told them. They gave him lots of goodbye cuddles and then they were off. Monkey watched them go, his eyes big and pleading.

'Don't worry, boy, they'll be back,' I told him, feeling so proud of how he had behaved. Monkey clearly had the perfect temperament for this job – now it was up to me to make sure he was ready for his scenes in time.

Chapter Nineteen

Training 9–5

With filming up at the main sets well under way, we were in the full swing of training down at our little HQ. The owls were finally making some progress, which was a relief. The team had also made good strides with a ferret we had recently acquired, which was needed for an important scene in which the teacher Mad-Eye Moody turns school bully Draco Malfoy into a rodent as punishment. Ferrets are quite intelligent, so very trainable, but they do have a nasty habit of giving their human handlers a little nip. Given that this ferret had to be trained to run up the trouser leg of the young actor Jamie Waylett, who played Vincent Crabbe, this was important to address! In conversation with the costume designers, we had already decided Jamie would wear two pairs of trousers, one which you'd see on camera, and one underneath to protect his skin. The ferret would very briefly run between the two – and he had to learn to do that without biting.

You see, it's not just dogs and cats that I work with: my team have a good go at training just about any animal a director sets their heart on. During the filming of the second *Harry Potter* film, *The Chamber of Secrets*, we needed to use live spiders for some of the scenes. So one day we took a delivery of two hundred tarantulas. I have to confess, I just couldn't go on set that day. Snakes, rats, cockroaches: all of these I can and have dealt with. But spiders – no. I just can't go near them. Luckily I was working with a very brave and ingenious group of trainers who were able to get the spiders to do what the director wanted!

I'm always up for a new challenge, but dogs and cats are my passion. So I was happy that I was working mainly with Monkey, Max and Crackerjack, alternating their sessions during our long days of training up at the studios. As you can imagine, cats are more temperamental than dogs, and there were times when my feline pupils would simply go on strike. But Monkey – he was always raring to go.

While I wouldn't exactly call him a model student – he was more the class clown – Monkey was picking up his tricks incredibly fast. His lust for life made him the perfect dog to work with, because he just found it all such tremendous fun. As soon as he saw me coming towards the dog run with my bait belt strapped on, he would start going mad with his eagerness to get going.

After the first few weeks of gentle relationship

building and short sessions, we had moved on to obedience work – going to a mark, walking to heel, coming when called. Once Monkey had mastered these, I started teaching the specific tricks he would need in his scenes. As the weeks went on, he learned how to walk backwards, crawl on his belly and lower his head in fear.

To do this last one, I first got Monkey to stand facing me. Then I would hold a treat in my hand and, giving the command 'down', I would lower it to the floor – of course Monkey's big head followed!

As soon as he started to lower his head I rewarded him with the treat. Gradually building on that, I got him to go down further, then to do it following just my hand movement, without a treat.

It is a move that can be a little tricky to teach, as the dog generally thinks they need to lie down. To correct this, I would pop my hand under Monkey's tummy so he knew it had to stay up from the floor. After a week working solidly on this trick, he had it sussed.

Hagrid describes Fang early on in the books as a 'big coward' – and that character was carried through to the films too. So, like the bowing head, a lot of the behaviour I taught Monkey, and Hugo before him, involved looking scared and submissive. It's kind of funny seeing such a big dog acting frightened of their own shadow. But in my experience, it often rings true. Just as lots of little dogs think they are bigger than they are and have a feisty personality to match, lots of big ones think they are small and vulnerable. That was certainly the case with Monkey. As poor Lisa could attest, he had decided he was a lapdog – and would often try and clamber onto her knee for a cuddle despite his enormous size!

There is one big change from the books, and that's what breed Fang is. J. K. Rowling described him as a boarhound, which is an old-fashioned term for any large dog bred for hunting. Lots of people interpret it to mean a Great Dane, but when it came to casting a dog for the films, breeds like the Irish wolfhound and Scottish deerhound were considered. Both those breeds are very tall and rangy, and at first glance look almost like wolves, which is why I think the Neapolitan mastiff was chosen instead. With their big heads and chunky bodies they are a commanding presence, and look quite threatening – although of course neither Fang, nor the dogs that played him, actually were.

Hugo had been pretty lazy, content to sleep for large portions of the day and only ready to rouse himself if there was a really tasty treat on offer. But Monkey couldn't have been more different. For such a large dog, he had an enormous amount of energy, and I had to fit in frequent walks around his training sessions. The other trainers and I came up with a clever solution to keep him well exercised without wearing ourselves out: we'd borrow one of the bikes the crew used to get around the vast complex and just cycle along,

Monkey bouncing alongside. With his long legs he covered a lot of ground and it was much easier to keep up with him by bike.

Every week I had to email a progress report to the director, and as the days whizzed by I found myself feeling more and more confident that Monkey would be able to deliver his scenes. What I was less sure about was how he would behave himself on set. He was very cheeky and had his mad moments – to me it was charming, but would it be as endearing to a busy film crew?

As usual I found the experience of gearing up for another *Harry Potter* absorbing, rewarding and exhausting. Every day brought new challenges, but it was too much fun to ever feel like work. By the end of the day I'd be more than ready to collapse on the sofa with Glenn, still chattering away about owls and ferrets and whatever mischief Monkey had got himself into. Glenn would always laugh and say my job was so ridiculous it might as well be made up.

Training 9–5

I had to agree, and I knew how lucky I was to live this crazy life, working with my beloved animals every day. The best part was seeing rescue animals like Monkey really nail it, and I was so proud of how far he'd come already. After two months with me he pretty much had all his tricks under his belt, which was just as well because his first scene, with Hagrid and Harry, was fast approaching. But the experience of being on set would be very different from the training ground and I wanted to help him prepare. With just two weeks left until he'd be on camera, I needed to take him on location. It was time to go deep into the Forbidden Forest.

Chapter Twenty

Into the Woods

I always like to introduce the animals to the location they'll be working in ahead of filming, so they get used to the environment. As in Monkey's case, I try to do it about a fortnight before the animal is due on set, so they already know the tricks they will need to do, but there's still time to do some work with them if there's anything about the location that alarms them.

That's especially important on a fantasy-type film like *Harry Potter*, where the set may be very unusual indeed.

Of course, it's not always possible to go to the set, either because it is still being built or it is at a location you don't have access to. In that scenario, I try to recreate the set environment as closely as possible instead. For example, when I was preparing Pickles for her first film, I knew she would have to run through a crowd of people. I couldn't risk her seeing a crowd for the first time on set, so Glenn helped me to get a load of my neighbours together so she could practise. It's this sort of attention to detail that ensures your animal remains calm and obedient when it matters.

Monkey's first scene was going to be shot at night, in the Forbidden Forest, and he'd be following Hagrid and Harry through the trees. Hagrid wants to show Harry the dragons he'll be expected to fight during the first task of the

Triwizard Tournament – and Fang gets scared when he catches a glimpse.

In reality, the Forbidden Forest wasn't as scary as it sounds. The scene would be shot at Black Park, a vast expanse of heath and woodland adjacent to Pinewood Studios in the Buckinghamshire countryside.

I wanted to take Monkey there when it was dark, so he'd get used to working in those conditions.

The park is generally open to the public when filming isn't taking place, but closes at 6 p.m. Luckily, I had a contact at Pinewood who could arrange for me to be let in after hours. Which was how Jo, Monkey and I found ourselves pulling up to the edge of the forest in the pitch black one Wednesday evening, ready for Monkey's first night-time training session.

Ed, my Pinewood contact, was waiting for us by the gates. Red-headed and wearing a green polo shirt, he unlocked the enormous padlock, holding the gate open for us. 'Good luck, Jules!' he said, giving Monkey a pat as we walked by. 'Just drop me a line when you're done and I'll come and lock up.'

We thanked Ed and pressed on into the woods, Jo holding up her torch. I had to admit, there was something quite spooky about this place in the dark. It was late – the longest day had just passed a week or so ago, so we had waited till after 10 p.m. for it to be properly pitch black. As our eyes adjusted, we could make out the path that wound through the trees, but the torch was casting strange shadows which seemed to leap and jump amid the crowded trunks. Beyond the yellow circle of light was a deep pool of blackness, where anything could be hiding. J. K. Rowling knew what she was doing when she made the Forbidden Forest the setting for many of the scarier scenes – there was definitely something unsettling about being among the trees at night.

When we actually came to film here it would

be very different, the woods bustling with people and with enormous studio lights. But for now, we were on our own.

'Bit creepy, isn't it?' said Jo, echoing my thoughts. Even Monkey was more subdued than normal as he padded along next to us. I pulled my jacket tighter around me and told myself my fears were all in my head.

Jo had a printed map in her hand, which she kept stopping to check. We were looking for the clearing where the dragons would be kept, and then we'd work backwards from there to figure out where Monkey's scene should begin.

After another five minutes of tripping over roots in the dark, we reached a spot where the trees opened up into a grassy space. 'Right, this is it,' Jo said, spinning the torchlight around the clearing. 'So I guess we'll be coming from that direction ...'

We paced back into the woods to where we planned to start, and I unclipped Monkey from his lead. He immediately trotted over to the nearest tree, cocked his leg and – well, you can imagine the rest. It was enough to break the tension, and Jo and I started laughing. 'The set is not meant to be a toilet, Monkey!' I joked.

Jo was going to be Hagrid, while I would stand a little way away, as if I was off camera, and give Monkey his commands. One of the hard things with training animals for films is teaching them to keep their eyes on their on-screen owner while still listening out for commands from their trainer. Automatically, they want to look at you, but that would obviously look weird on camera. I had been teaching Monkey how to do this up at the training centre, roping in various different trainers to be Hagrid so he got used to doing it with lots of people.

Monkey just had to walk at Hagrid's heels through the woods, then when he saw the dragon he would lower his head and back away.

Once Monkey realised we were doing some

training, he was as happy and energetic as always. The dark didn't seem to bother him – dogs can see much better in low light than humans, which probably helped – and he was soon running through his scene like a pro. I noticed that when he lowered his head he was getting a little distracted by the exciting sticks on the ground, and you could almost see the cogs turning in his head as he resisted the urge to pick one up and run away with it. I was so proud of how focused he was on his training.

Once we'd run through the scene several times without a hitch, Jo and I decided to call it a night. I yawned – I'd been up at 7 a.m. as usual with the dogs and it had been a long day. Monkey didn't seem tired at all, however, so we left him off the lead so he could have a final stretch of his legs on the way back to the gate.

'Here, have half of this,' said Jo, producing a Mars bar from her jacket pocket. I gratefully accepted, and we stopped for a moment as she carefully split it in two. In the distance, I heard a rustle, and then before we even had time to react Monkey was sprinting away from us, thundering through the undergrowth.

'Monkey!' I yelled. 'Come back here!' The rustling must have been a rabbit or a squirrel, and now Monkey had gone tearing off into the dark woods after it. I tried again, 'Come, come, come, Monkey, come!', but to no avail.

Jo and I sprinted in the direction Monkey had headed in, but the sound of him leaping through the bracken was getting more and more distant. How do you find a dark grey dog in a pitch-black wood in the middle of the night? 'Monkey!' I called, more desperately this time. 'Monkey!'

We pressed on, slower now that we had lost the path and had to be careful not to twist our ankles. People often make the mistake of thinking all my animals are perfectly behaved. That is simply not true. Many of them have a real naughty streak – because, weirdly, animals who are a bit cheeky and mischievous are often the ones that respond best to training. Just because they can do their tricks perfectly doesn't mean they don't still have a bit of wilfulness that makes them choose to ignore the rules when it suits them.

'Oh God, this is such a nightmare,' I said to Jo, panic rising in my stomach. Monkey's recall had been perfect lately; if it hadn't been, I would never have had him off the lead. But despite calling him and using the whistle he wasn't returning. He was clearly so distracted all his training had gone out the window.

'Don't worry, he'll come back,' Jo said, but there was uncertainty in her voice.

We stopped and Jo slowly shone her torch around us, searching for any sign of Monkey. 'There!' I said. I'd spotted a movement among the trees to our left, and it was getting closer . . .

All of a sudden, Monkey leapt from the thicket and threw himself at Jo and me, full of happiness to see us again. I was so relieved he'd come back and quickly clipped him on to the lead, giving him a treat so he knew he'd done the right thing by returning. My heart was still racing; he'd only disappeared for a matter of minutes but it had been long enough to feel like a lifetime. What if he did it on set?

'Thank goodness for that!' said Jo. 'Now let's get the hell out of here ...'

That was easier said than done, as we hadn't really paid attention when we had left the path. After a lot of stumbling around, we eventually found our way back to the track. I texted Ed, telling him we'd be at the gate in five minutes.

He was waiting for us when we got there, his car engine running and headlights beaming. 'That was longer than I expected,' said Ed, his eyes taking in our muddy trainers and the bits of twig I could now see were tucked behind Monkey's ears. 'Everything go OK in there?'

'Thank you so much for staying so late, Ed,' I said. 'I really am sorry for keeping you hanging on. Let's just say, this one is a Monkey by name and monkey by nature.'

Ed laughed. 'No further questions!'

I could laugh it off, but our escapade in the woods worried me. Monkey had been great in training, but there were clearly still some distractions he couldn't resist. A film set would potentially be full of them. Would he be able to keep his focus and be the star I knew he could be?

Chapter Twenty-One

Ready or Not

With the first day of filming drawing ever closer, I had to hope Monkey had got his moment of madness out of his system. To be fair to him, over the next fortnight he was as good as gold. I couldn't really blame him for getting over-excited in the woods, but I was a little anxious that he was going to be totally hyper when he found himself on an actual film set.

We were on schedule: having learned all his moves, Monkey had progressed to running through his specific scenes every day, with the other trainers stepping in as 'actors' to make it as close to the real experience as possible.

Three days before filming, I invited Lisa up to the training ground to see Monkey in action. She clapped with delight as she watched her baby run through his scenes flawlessly.

'He's so clumsy most of the time, I was finding it hard to imagine him performing on cue,' she told me afterwards. 'But I can see now he's a natural!' Her enthusiasm was the confidence boost I needed.

The following day, it was time to introduce Monkey to his co-stars: the two Hagrids. Yes, you read that right – during the filming of *Harry Potter*, two people played the Hogwarts game-keeper. You are probably thinking of Robbie Coltrane, who was the lead actor. But there was also his body double Martin Bayfield, an ex-England rugby player, who at nearly seven feet tall stood in for Robbie for shots in which it was necessary to emphasise Hagrid's unusual size. Martin, who also played a young Hagrid in *The Chamber of Secrets*, often ended up shooting scenes with Fang, which as a dog lover he was more than happy about. I loved working with both him and Robbie, who was always so funny and cheerful.

I had arranged to meet them at the tables outside the central canteen one lunchtime. With Monkey by my side, I headed towards the main set through the maze of trailers that belonged to the cast and crew. It was a warm day, with many people sunning themselves outside, and everyone wanted to greet Monkey as he went past. It meant our progress was slow, and by the time I reached the canteen Martin and Robbie were already there.

As you can imagine, they were not hard to spot. Robbie must have been filming that day, because he was wearing Hagrid's bushy black wig and enormous beard. He once told me that it took the hair and make-up crew two hours to get him looking like Hagrid, and at the end of the day a team of people would literally scrub the beard off with hot oil. On top of that, his heavy costume, made of imitation fur cleverly cut to look like mole pelts, weighed a sweltering 30kg. The wardrobe department had designed it with special tubes in its vest and sleeves, so they could pour in cold water to stop him from sweating. It sounded terribly uncomfortable – not that Robbie would ever complain, because he loved the part.

It didn't look like Martin had been on camera that day because he was clean shaven and dressed casually in a T-shirt and jeans, but his enormous height meant that he stood out just as much as Robbie. They were sitting at one of the metal tables, steaming plates of sausage and mash in front of them, Martin uncomfortably folded into a chair that was far too small for him.

Robbie spotted us first and started waving. I waved back, leading Monkey over to the table.

By now Robbie was on his feet, ready to say hello to his on-screen pet. But Monkey's attention was elsewhere: on the sausage and mash. My heart sank.

There's no getting away from the fact that with Neapolitan mastiffs, slobber is an issue. The moment there was a treat on offer, Monkey would start drooling. I always carried a towel with me, ready to quickly wipe it away before he shook his head, sending slobber flying everywhere. It seemed that today Monkey had decided he quite fancied Martin and Robbie's lunch. I didn't want him to shake his head and cover the two of them – and their food – with drool before they had even had a chance to get acquainted.

'Hi Robbie, hi Martin – bear with me one second,' I greeted them, rummaging in my bag for the towel and quickly giving Monkey a clean-up. When I straightened up I saw them both chuckling. After three films, they were used to the necessity of the slobber towel.

Martin gave me a quick kiss on the cheek, then Robbie pulled me into a hug, his beard tickling my neck. 'Good to see you again, Jules. And another handsome boy you've got for us!'

I could tell both he and Martin were delighted to meet Monkey, whose daft exuberance was impossible to resist. I glowed with pleasure – I'm always happy when anyone loves my animals even a fraction of the amount I do.

We chatted through the scene, which was going to involve some long shots of Martin with Fang, as well as some tighter frames of Robbie. 'Looks like he's going to enjoy working with both of you,' I laughed, as Martin sneaked an extremely grateful Monkey a bit of sausage from his plate.

With our meet-and-greet done, it was time for Monkey to take it easy before filming. The evening before the big day, Lisa and Monkey joined me and my little pack of dogs for a final walk around the Tring reservoirs. It had become one of Monkey's favourite places, and he loved nothing more than tearing ahead with Ginelli and Lala in a mad game of chase. After all his hard work, it felt good to see him so happy.

'It's hard to believe he's the same dog you brought up here that first day, isn't it?' said Lisa, as Monkey joyfully belly-flopped into the water, sending a tsunami over little Pickles, who was watching on the bank.

It was true: Monkey was now the picture of health, his body thick and muscular and his coat shining with an amazing blue-grey lustre. Before I'd rescued him, he had been starved not just of food but of affection too, but with lots of care and kindness his true personality, as the ultimate people-pleaser, had shone through.

From the very first day I had known how special he was, and throughout our twelve weeks of training he had lived up to that promise. Managing my team of trainers and getting such a huge variety of animals ready had been hard work, but having Monkey by my side had lightened the load every day. He seemed to always know when I was stressed and would do something daft to distract me, or when I was weary he'd plonk himself down beside me for some fuss, giving me an excuse for a breather. Some days I felt like I couldn't do it without him.

I was so grateful for this wonderful dog who had burst into our lives with so much love to give. He had gone from unruly rescue to a well-trained and beloved pet in just under three months. It was such a short time, and I had to hope we had done enough. Tomorrow our hard work would be put to the test.

Chapter Twenty-Two

Picture Perfect

Finally, the big day was upon us. Most days on set start notoriously early, so my alarm would usually be set for 5 a.m. But this was different. We wouldn't be filming until it was dark, so our call time for the set at Black Park wasn't until the late afternoon.

That gave me plenty of time to get Monkey looking camera ready. Lisa dropped him off around midday, and I took him up to the training HQ. I wanted to keep his routine fairly regular so he'd be calm and relaxed by the time he was due on set.

Now it was time to get him looking his best. Grooming is something I'm pretty good at, having spent the early part of my career working in a doggy hairdresser's. I knew from an early age that I wanted to work with animals, and my dreams fixed on the grooming parlour, Mucky Pups, which was round the corner from my family home in Harrow, north London.

At fourteen I got a Saturday job there and immediately loved it. I got to spend all day with different dogs – what could be better? So as soon as I could leave school I did, and started working at the groomer's full time. Some dogs absolutely adore being pampered but I quickly learned that for some of them it can be a frightening experience. I loved finding different ways to keep the various dogs calm and relaxed. I realised that if you could work out what makes an animal tick you could find a way to make them trust you. Even the trickiest canine customers would eventually stand obediently while I washed and groomed them – you just had to be gentle and patient.

It was a lesson I'd carried through into my career as a trainer, and I truly believe that the work I did at the groomer's was like a college education in animal behaviour. And, of course, it meant I was a dab hand with the clippers and brush.

Neapolitan mastiffs have short, shedding coats, so they don't need as much grooming as some breeds. But this was no ordinary occasion. Monkey, who loved to dive into the muddiest ditches or roll in the smelliest cow pats, was used to being hosed down, but today I planned for him to have a proper bath.

At our HQ I had a big tub specifically for that purpose, which we kept in one of the empty concrete-floored rooms in the kennel block. It was an old steel bath but wasn't connected to the mains, so I had to go back and forth with a bucket, filling it up with lukewarm water. Monkey, stretched out in a patch of sunlight near the outside tap, watched me with one eyebrow raised.

Once the bath was full, I fetched my grooming kit and went to get Monkey. I gave him a quick brush to get the loosest hairs out of his coat, then led him to the bath.

Monkey didn't need much persuading to jump in. He hit the water with such force that half of it immediately splashed out over the sides and all over my trainers. So much for all that careful fetching and carrying!

With Monkey's tail flapping madly and creating mini tidal waves, I knew I had to act fast before the bath was emptied completely. I soaped him all over with special doggy shampoo and he wriggled with happiness. I somehow knew he would enjoy bath time – it was a chance to make a mess and get lots of attention, which alongside food were his favourite things.

I dipped the bucket in the bath water and poured it gently over his back to rinse off the shampoo. I had a soft flannel tucked into my back pocket and I now pulled it out, carefully lifting up the folds of Monkey's wrinkly face and wiping underneath to make sure every part of him was clean.

When I was done, Monkey hopped out of the bath and gave an almighty shake. I was pretty much as sodden as he was, so it was just as well I had packed a change of clothes!

I put Monkey in the dog run to steam off in the sun. Once he was just about dry, I distracted him with a scrap of ham to get him to stand still, then used a grooming mitt to massage him all over in a circular motion. This helps to stimulate the release of natural oils and get rid of any remaining loose hairs. Once that was done, I gave him a spritz with a hydrating spray, to lock in moisture and ensure his coat was as glossy and shiny as could be.

'Don't you look handsome, Monkey?' I said, standing back to admire my handiwork. He definitely looked the part. But with this cheeky dog, the challenge would be ensuring he was still as clean and tidy by the time we headed to set. Luckily, it seemed his thoughts had turned to cuddles rather than rolling in mud, and he snuggled his head into my lap for a stroke. I still needed to pack my bag, get my script notes, read through the shooting plan once more ... but I couldn't resist stopping for some quality time with Monkey.

As Monkey's eyes grew heavy and he settled himself for a nap, I glanced at my watch – just an hour to go. It was nearly showtime.

Chapter Twenty-Three

Back to Black Park

When it was finally time to head up to Black Park, I loaded Monkey into the back of my Mitsubishi Shogun. He must have assumed we were going home as usual, so when we pulled into the car park at the woods he scrambled to his feet and pressed his nose to the window, eagerly taking in this surprising new location with his big brown eyes.

I popped the back door open and Monkey jumped out, his body quivering a little with anticipation. There were already lots of cars and vans here and the noise of the crew wheeling cameras into place and shouting instructions to one another was carrying over the tall pine trees. He could sense there was some fun to be had.

'It's your big moment, Monkey!' I whispered to him as I hoisted the bag of his treats, toys and brushes onto my back.

'Julie, hi!' called a voice. It was Abi, a runner who had also worked on the last film. Her fair hair piled on her head in a messy bun, she was dressed in a black vest, shorts, and Timberland boots, a hoodie slung round her waist for when it got cooler later. 'We've got a trailer set up for you guys over here: let me show you.'

Film productions don't travel light – especially not *Harry Potter.* It was like someone had picked up half the main film set and moved it down the road to Black Park. There were trailers for everyone who would be needed – we passed by hair and make-up, wardrobe and visual effects before we reached ours. Most of the crew had been here all day setting up the scene and making sure lights, cameras and microphones were all positioned perfectly.

'They're just finishing getting set up,' Abi was saying. 'I'll come and get you when they're ready for you. You know about the dragon, right?'

'I do,' I replied eagerly. 'The creature effects department gave me a full run-down earlier in the week. I can't wait to see the finished product!'

The *Harry Potter* films might be all about magic, but the real wizardry takes place off camera. In this film, Harry had to fight a Hungarian Horntail dragon as part of the Triwizard Tournament. As with every single detail in the *Potter* universe, a huge amount of thought and discussion went into the design for the dragon. In the fight scene, which sees the Horntail chase Harry on his broom from the tournament arena over the mountains and through the turrets and spires of Hogwarts Castle, the dragon was entirely created from CGI. But before that could be done, the art department had to draw endless versions of the dragon until a final design was approved. After that, sculptors made a full-size model of the dragon's head, complete with hawk-like features, razor-sharp teeth and a crown of vicious-looking spikes. The model was needed as a lighting reference when creating the CGI.

But for this scene in the forest, creature effect supervisor Nick Dudman and special effects head John Richardson didn't think CGI was going to cut it. They wanted a forty-foot dragon – and with the head already in place, the creature shop just had to build the body and tail. The idea was to create an enormous puppet, which would be silhouetted in its cage. It would be able to realistically shake and rattle its bars while Harry and Hagrid looked on.

I'd had all this explained to me by the creature effects department, whose work always blew me away. Proving that nothing ever went to waste on

the *Potter* set, they had repurposed the Basilisk,
a giant snake, from the second film, to make
the body and wings of the dragon. Crew members would hide under the wings to flap them
about and make the Horntail move. The *pièce de
résistance* was when special effects put a flame-
thrower in its mouth; it could apparently throw
fire thirty feet, controlled via a computer system. I
had been reassured that no flame-throwing would
happen while Monkey was on set, which was a
relief – it sounded a bit frightening for a dog.

The dragon was certainly a pretty special prop,
with so much time, ingenuity and resources lav-
ished on it. So it wasn't exactly something I could
just borrow to practise with Monkey. He'd be
seeing it for the first time on set. He was a confident dog and he trusted me, so I was sure I could
keep him calm. But I hoped seeing a life-size
dragon wouldn't prove too much of a distraction
and cause him not to come when I called.

Once we reached our trailer, Abi bid us

farewell, telling us we'd be needed in about an hour and a half. There's always a lot of waiting around on set, so I was grateful for the trailer, which had a little built-in kitchen at one end with everything I needed to make endless cups of tea. I unpacked Monkey's things, laying out a fluffy blanket on the floor next to the narrow floral sofa and pouring some water into his bowl. I peered out of the window – darkness was falling rapidly, so it wouldn't be long until conditions were right.

Monkey settled himself down for a snooze as I put the kettle on. I checked my phone: good luck messages had pinged in from Jo, Lisa and Glenn. 'I'll wait up for you,' Glenn wrote. 'There's a celebratory bottle of champagne in the fridge!' I smiled, and typed back: 'Don't jinx it!!!' No matter how well prepared you feel – and I had every faith in Monkey – animals are ultimately unpredictable, so you never know how things are going to pan out.

He was, after all, a rescue dog, and I didn't

know the ins and outs of his past. Who knows what triggers I hadn't yet discovered. I trusted him completely, but I've never taken an animal on set for the first time without feeling a little anxious. I so desperately wanted Monkey to do well and enjoy himself.

Curling up on the sofa, I pulled out my copy of the script, covered in my scrawled training notes, and read through the scene for the millionth time. I knew it by heart, of course, but it calmed my nerves to go over and over it in my mind.

Eventually, there was a knock on the trailer door. By now, it was pitch black outside, with just a handful of stars in the velvety sky. I opened the door, pumping with adrenalin, to find Abi standing on the steps, clipboard in hand.

'Can you and Monkey come with me please, Julie,' she said. 'It's time.'

Chapter Twenty-Four

Enter the Dragon

I gulped – it was the moment of truth. 'Monkey!' I called, and he was on his feet immediately. I clipped on my bait belt – his favourite treats of sausage and chicken stowed inside – and put Monkey on his lead.

We followed Abi past the rest of the trailers and down a pathway through the woods, which had been lit with strings of lights so you could see exactly where you were going. Not that we really needed it: through the trees I could see spotlights on massive rigs blazing away.

Abi led us to the spot in the woods where our scene would start. As usual on a film set, it was a hubbub of people, all intent on their individual jobs. The gaffer, in charge of the colour and intensity of light, was barking instructions at his team, who were making tiny adjustments until the ghostly blue glow of the Forbidden Forest was just right. I could see the grips fiddling around with a dolly, which the camera had been attached to. The boom operator, his microphone on a pole leant casually against his shoulder, was chatting to one of the sound mixers. Huddled under a gazebo, two assistant directors were deep in conversation with the director, Mike Newell, no doubt finalising their plan of attack. And right in the centre of it all was Harry Potter, aka Daniel Radcliffe, a woman armed with a can of hairspray tweaking his messy dark hair. He grinned when he saw me, raising his hand in greeting.

Then, something caught my eye and made me gasp. About a hundred yards from where we stood was the clearing we had been to on our practice run, and in the centre of it was a massive cage, containing the most realistic-looking dragon I had ever seen. Through the bars I could make out its raptor-like face, jaws open to reveal gleaming teeth. The dragon was crouched, but it was still at least seven feet tall. Its black scales glinted bronze in the beaming lights that had been positioned to illuminate it perfectly. Bat-like wings were folded into its side, and massive talons gripped the edge of the cage. If I didn't know better, I'd have sworn it was real.

'Go and have a closer look!' urged Abi. 'You've got time.'

I didn't need telling twice. With Monkey's lead gripped in my hands, I slowly approached, marvelling at the genius of the creature department.

Nick Dudman – carefully parted salt-and-pepper hair, square glasses and a warm smile – spotted me. 'Hi Julie! You're just in time to see the dragon in action.'

I could see black-clad members of his crew

climbing into the cage. 'They'll be hidden inside, making it move,' he told me. 'Just watch – this should be great.' Even in the half-light I could see pride lighting up his face, and rightly so: the dragon was an incredible feat of artistry and engineering.

'OK, go!' he called. Suddenly the whole cage was trembling as the dragon swung from side to side, its massive wings unfurling. Transfixed, I had let Monkey's lead go loose in my hand – and too late I realised the Monkey madness was striking.

He barked joyfully, and suddenly he was plunging towards the dragon, yanking the lead straight out of my hand. 'Monkey!' I yelled desperately. Overbalancing, I stumbled and fell to my knees, and suddenly I saw the scene from Monkey's perspective. The dragon was simply the biggest toy he had ever encountered, and he wanted to play with it. This incredibly expensive, intricately designed, centrally important prop was about to become my dog's new plaything.

It was as if everything was moving in slow motion. Nick's face dropped in horror as Monkey bounced towards the dragon, which suddenly became ungainly as the puppet operators inside panicked. People up at the main set, a little way from the clearing, had wheeled round when they heard the commotion, and I could hear hurried footsteps. I was on my feet again, desperately grabbing for the lead.

'Monkey, stay!' I yelled at the top of my lungs. He was inches from the dragon's foot, his eyes locked on its meaty leg. His powerful jaws were open, ready to clamp around and wrestle with it, just as he would with one of his toys. But there must have been something in my voice that made him pause. He stopped in his tracks, and turned round to gaze at me with an innocent look on his face which said: 'What?'

I could feel my heart hammering in my throat, but I tried to keep my voice calm and authoritative. 'Monkey, sit!' He plonked his bottom down, but turned his eyes back hungrily to the dragon. Now I was close enough to grab his lead, and it was only once it was wrapped around my hands that I started to breathe again. I gave him a treat, said 'Heel, Monkey,' and began to pull him gently but firmly away from the dragon.

You could have heard a pin drop in the silence that followed. Finally, Nick let out his breath in a low whistle. 'Nick, I am so sorry,' I said. 'That was – I mean – I shouldn't – I didn't realise . . . I am just so sorry.'

Nick's shoulders started to shake, and my blood went cold – how angry was he? But then I realised he was laughing. Silently at first, then big guffaws. It seemed his laughing was infectious. The dragon operating team, emerging tentatively from the cage, were giggling too. Laughter rippled across the set, and Monkey looked up, puzzled, into my face, which set me off too.

Wiping the tears away from his eyes, Nick clapped a friendly hand to my shoulder. 'Well, that was a close call!' he said, shaking his head. 'But no harm done. Maybe the dragon isn't so scary after all, if a dog thinks he can take it on!'

'That's Monkey for you, I'm afraid,' I said ruefully. 'He just loves to play.'

'I reckon he might love you more, though,' shrugged Nick, still smiling. 'He stopped, didn't he, when you told him to?'

I looked down at Monkey, who was gazing up at me with puppy-dog eyes full of adoration. I think he could tell I was cross with him, but suddenly I realised I had no reason to be. He had only been doing what came naturally to him, and the moment I gave him the commands he had spent so long learning, he had obeyed. When it mattered, he hadn't let me down.

'You're a good boy really, aren't you?' I said, reaching into my bait belt for a treat. Monkey gobbled up the chicken gratefully, but he was even happier when I ruffled his ears. 'Just no more playing with dragons, OK?'

Enter the Dragon

I said goodbye to Nick, and headed back to where the crew were waiting to start shooting. Monkey had got everyone's attention, for all the wrong reasons. Now it was time to prove he wasn't just the class clown, but a star pupil.

Chapter Twenty-Five

Action!

'Never work with children and animals, they say!'

It was Robbie, who had arrived just in time to see the chaos unfold. Next to him stood Martin, also in full beard and costume. It always made me laugh to see them together like this – Martin towering head and shoulders over Robbie, their sweeping fur coats and tangled black hair identical.

'Wish someone had told me that before I made it my career,' I joked.

'Julie!' a voice called, and I spun back round to

see Mike Newell approaching. He was tall and jovial, wearing his signature waistcoat open over a checked shirt, his eyes twinkling behind wire-rimmed specs. 'Lovely to see you and, er . . .?'

'Monkey,' I supplied.

'How . . . appropriate,' said Mike, raising an eyebrow.

'Yes, sorry about that,' I said quickly. 'But he can't wait to get started now – can you, Monks?' He wagged his tail in agreement, looking like butter wouldn't melt.

'Good, good,' said Mike, turning back to the set. He pointed – 'So we'll need him there to start off with, then it's just a simple case of following Martin and Daniel for the long shot from behind. Then we'll do it again, just Robbie and Daniel, with close-ups.'

'Got it,' I said. It should all be nice and straightforward – as long as Monkey didn't decide to go off for another midnight run or dragon-fighting mission, that is.

I fished a scrap of sausage out of the bait belt and Monkey suddenly became super-alert. He loved training, and to him it made no difference that we were on this strangely surreal film set; he just relished the chance to please me and win himself a treat.

The assistant directors were busy clearing people from the set and getting Dan and Martin into position. There would be no dialogue in this shot: the actors would simply walk, with Monkey slinking along behind.

After Monkey had a quick pat from Dan and Martin, I got him into position using a mark, and gave him the command to keep his eyes on Martin.

'Action!' called Mike. Everyone started moving, including the camera, sliding smoothly along on the dolly tracks. I kept pace with Monkey, telling him 'walk, walk, walk' so he knew what was expected. I saw his ears flicker as he realised the camera was following him, but his attention never wavered from Martin's back. As he padded along in perfect time, I could feel pride swelling in my chest.

'And cut!' came the call.

'Clever boy!' I praised Monkey immediately, giving him the treat he'd been longing for, and a big hug.

Some tweaks were made to the lighting and then we were going again – and again, and again, and again. Most shots have to be taken several times so that the director has multiple angles to choose from. Monkey didn't seem to mind, patiently performing over and over, never putting a foot wrong.

'Great stuff!' Mike called when they had what they needed in the bag. I felt so relieved – Monkey had redeemed himself after the dragon incident.

Next it was time to shoot some close-ups of Monkey, who had to look frightened, lowering his head in fear and backing away. Lighting and the special effects team would do some clever work so that it looked like the fire breathed by the dragon was lighting up his face.

The professional lighting was all new to Monkey, but he took it in his stride. We had practised these moves so many times and now he'd perfected them. There was something about his expressive face that meant he really performed: he genuinely looked scared, rather than like a dog running through the motions that were meant to signal fear. I could hear a murmur go round the rapt crew as they watched my little star act his socks off.

It's hard to put into words the emotions I feel when I watch a dog like Monkey, who had such an unpromising start in life, impress the top people on a film set. Poor Monkey was a write-off – neglected, unloved and eventually dumped. His former owner had done him one final injustice by lying about his temperament, claiming he was aggressive when nothing could be further from the truth. If I hadn't been looking for a Neapolitan mastiff at that exact moment I may never have found him, and this beautiful animal could still be languishing in a shelter now. But here he was, performing alongside some of the most famous actors in the world, and nailing his scenes.

I have been known to cry on a film set, and I could feel a lump rising in my throat now as Monkey and I ran through the tricks again, so the camera could film a different angle. His concentration never wavered, and he seemed to know what I wanted before I even gave a command. It was as if Monkey and I were the only ones here – nothing else mattered.

Eventually, Mike had everything he needed and Monkey and I were free to go. As we left, the director came over to give Monkey a pat. 'I'm looking forward to seeing him again already,' he said.

'I think the feeling's mutual,' I replied, as Monkey predictably rolled over in a gesture of soppy submission.

Waving goodbye to the rest of the crew, I led Monkey to the car so I could drive him back to Lisa's. He gave a massive yawn as I settled him into his crate.

One day down, but there were plenty more to go. It was a great start, though, and I couldn't be prouder of my cheeky Monkey.

Chapter Twenty-Six

Pottermania

Monkey had earned a break. I never overwork my animals and always make sure they have the rest periods they need. Animals are just like humans: if they're tired, they can be grumpy and won't perform to the best of their abilities.

Lisa and I arranged for Monkey to have three days off, during which she took him for lots of walks to his favourite places and played plenty of silly games with him to keep his mind active. I was used to not seeing Monkey at the weekend anyway, but even one extra day away from him and I found myself missing his antics. He could always put a smile on my face with his clumsy, exuberant lust for life, and it felt weird heading to the studio without him.

But I didn't have to miss him for long, as there were several scenes coming up that called for Monkey. The first time he saw me again after his little break, I thought he was going to pass out with excitement. He started bouncing up and down, whining, running back and forth before throwing himself into my arms, unable to contain himself. 'Oh Monkey,' I told him, burying my face in his fur. 'I'm so happy to see you too.'

Over the next few weeks, we filmed several times alongside the Hagrids. In most of the shots, Monkey was in the background, and didn't have to do anything too complicated, but he was a hit with everyone.

In between takes I'd let him off his lead and he would run wild figures-of-eight around the set, bouncing around and jumping up to everybody. With other dogs I might have worried they were being a nuisance, but Monkey was so lovely with everyone he met, and so universally adored, that I knew no one minded. If things were getting a bit stressful you could always rely on Monkey to ease the tension, picking up stray props like discarded wands and running around with them, tripping over his own feet, or chasing his tail. With his gangly legs all over the place he looked absolutely bonkers, like a puppet whose strings had been cut. But as soon as the call came for action he'd focus immediately, always performing perfectly when it mattered.

It was a joy to see how much Monkey loved being on set, especially if there were children there. I quickly realised he had a real affinity for the kids. They were his favourite playmates, and he'd do anything to get five minutes with one of the younger cast members.

As word spread about Monkey, we rapidly

gained a steady stream of visitors down at our training HQ. Young actors who were struggling with their school work, or had fallen out with a friend, would come and have a much-needed cuddle with Monkey to make themselves feel better. It was as if he had a sixth sense for when someone needed comfort, and instead of being the goofy joker he would be gentle and loving. I'd sometimes catch one of the kids leaning against Monkey's bulky form, pouring out their hearts to him, and sneak away quietly to leave them to it. I reckon he must have been a very good listener.

Two months rolled by, and before I knew it September had arrived and it was time for Monkey's final scene, set inside Hagrid's hut. While the exterior of Hagrid's lodge-like home was shot on location in Glencoe, Scotland, the interior was carefully constructed in the studio at Leavesden. The brilliant set designers had created a snug home which fitted Hagrid's personality perfectly, with lots of cosy rugs and a cluttered dresser full of crockery, while baskets and cages for magical creatures were stacked in every corner and hanging from the ceiling. There was a squashy leather armchair and a rough-hewn kitchen table, around which Harry, Ron and Hermione would arrange themselves when they came to visit.

Monkey was excited to find himself on this set, as most of his previous work had been done outside. I let him have a good sniff around the place when we first arrived and I could see him making himself at home – just like Fang.

'This is your last scene, buddy, so make it count!' I told him. He wagged his tail happily.

To be honest, I expected the whole thing to be a breeze for Monkey. All he had to do was stay lying by the fire while Daniel and Robbie – or Harry and Hagrid, I should say – chatted at the kitchen table. But I suppose I should have learned by now that with Monkey it's best to expect the unexpected.

Once all the cast were in position, and Monkey was lying obediently on his rug, Mike called

'Action!' As the cameras rolled the actors performed their lines while I stood just off set with a piece of sausage in my hand, giving Monkey the command to stay. But the scene was quite long, and Monkey was getting more and more eager for the treat. How could I tell? Those tell-tale trails of drool, of course.

I had the slobber towel in my hand, poised to clean him up the moment 'Cut!' was called. But when it eventually was, I couldn't get to Monkey. The space was tight and crowded, and with make-up rushing on to powder Robbie's nose, Daniel trying to get out for a glass of water, and one of the technicians trying to move a light, my way to Monkey was blocked.

With all the commotion going on around him, Monkey got lazily to his feet. I could see him looking for me, and the sausage. But finding there was an impenetrable crowd of people around him, he decided to shake his head instead.

It was just about the worst thing he could have

done in the confined space. The drool splattered everywhere – all over Robbie's bespoke hand-made costume, onto every surface of the perfectly designed cabin, and coating the make-up artist's shoes. There were gasps of horror as I rushed in, seconds too late, towel in hand.

'Sorry, everybody,' I said ruefully. 'Just an occupational hazard, I'm afraid . . .'

Luckily no one in the *Harry Potter* team was so precious they would get annoyed at a dog, but I knew the wardrobe department and the set designers weren't too pleased as they hastily scrubbed dog drool from their works of art.

It seemed a fitting way to finish Monkey's time on *The Goblet of Fire*. He'd been a true professional throughout – but with a healthy dose of Monkey madness thrown in to keep things interesting. I felt a little sad as I clipped him onto his lead, knowing it was the last scene we would shoot together for a while. It had that feeling of a school year coming to a close: happy exhaustion after all that hard work, but a sense of nostalgia too.

'You've done me proud, boy,' I told Monkey as we walked back down towards the training ground, the late-afternoon autumn sun casting long shadows. I still had some scenes to oversee in the next few weeks, but for Monkey this would be his last day at Leavesden. I already knew it would feel very quiet without him.

When I arrived back at our HQ, I was surprised to see Jo and the rest of the team waiting for me outside the Portakabin – I thought they would have already started heading home.

'What are you all doing here?' I asked them. Then I spotted the bottles of cava and plastic cups – we were celebrating!

Jo pulled a package wrapped in brown paper from behind her back with a flourish and tossed it to Monkey. 'Graduation present!' she announced as Monkey delightedly tore it open to find a chewy rope toy inside. 'We couldn't let Monkey's last day on his first movie go unmarked.'

I grinned and took a cup of fizz from Guillaume, then started regaling my team with the tale of Monkey's slobber tsunami at Hagrid's hut. He weaved happily among our legs saying hello to everyone, as if he knew this was his party. Eventually he came to sit regally at my side, and I laid my head on my faithful friend's forehead. How I was going to miss having him beside me!

Working on a *Potter* film is always an intense process, and then it's done almost before you realise it. *The Goblet of Fire* was no different. Ten days later, I had finished too, and found myself catapulted back into the reality of life outside the *Potter* bubble.

The film wouldn't be released until 2005, and I would have to wait until then to see which, if any, of Monkey's scenes made the final cut. *Harry Potter* is such a mammoth project and they always shoot much more than they need, so plenty of scenes end up on the cutting-room floor.

What I did know for certain, however, was that we would be back in 2006 for the next instalment of the series, *Harry Potter and the Order of the Phoenix*. The production team had already signed me up, and Monkey had done so well everyone wanted him to return as Fang.

Lisa was more than happy to give Monkey a home until then. I knew I was going to really miss working with him on a daily basis, but as I saw Lisa most days I would still get plenty of time with my crazy canine pal. There was no question that I wanted him to keep working as Fang for as long as he could.

Little did I know there was a crisis on the horizon – which would rock even the best-made plans.

Chapter Twenty-Seven

Code Blue

The day of disaster began like any other Saturday. It was late September 2005, about a year since *The Goblet of Fire* wrapped. The days were getting shorter and the leaves on the trees starting to turn, but summer seemed determined to hang on for one last hurrah. August had been drizzly and disappointing, and it was as if the sun had decided to come out at the last minute, before winter descended.

Glenn and I had made the most of the good

weather by taking the dogs on a four-hour walk across the Chiltern Hills, marvelling at the golden fields, freshly harvested, and greedily picking plump blackberries from the thriving hedgerows. Back at the cottage we slumped on sun loungers with cold cans of Coke, while the dogs flopped on the grass, exhausted.

The steady breathing of my snoozing pets, the warmth of the afternoon rays and the gentle sounds of turtledoves cooing from the cottage gables meant that it wasn't long before I felt my eyelids grow heavy. I'm always on the go and relaxing doesn't come that easily to me, but after a busy week's training I decided to surrender. I was just about to nod off when the shrill ringing of the phone coming through the open kitchen door jolted me awake.

I sat up, disorientated. 'Just leave it,' said Glenn sleepily from the lounger next to me. 'If it's important they'll ring back.'

I hesitated, tempted to lie back down and

recapture the feeling of intense relaxation from just moments before. But what if it was about one of my animals? I knew I couldn't ignore it.

The phone was still ringing – whoever was on the other end was pretty determined to speak to me. Jamming my feet back into my discarded trainers, I hurried inside and dived for the receiver before it rung off.

'Hello?'

'Julie, thank God!' It was Lisa, and I could tell at once something was seriously wrong. She sounded breathless and panicked, as if she was on the verge of bursting into tears.

'Lisa, what's wrong? It's OK, just breathe, tell me what's happened.'

On the other end, I heard Lisa gulp for air. 'It's Monkey,' she said. 'I think he's got bloat. He needs to go to the vet but he's so heavy I can't lift him.'

I felt dread slice through me like the cold blade of a knife. If Monkey really did have bloat, we had just minutes to act. Even if we were fast, he might not survive.

'Wait right there,' I said, trying to sound calmer than I felt. 'We'll be there as soon as we can.'

Slamming the receiver down, I yelled into the garden for Glenn. 'We need to go to Lisa's right now! Monkey's in trouble.'

The distress in my voice roused Glenn faster than any alarm could. Within seconds he was herding the dogs inside and grabbing the car keys.

'I'll drive,' he said as we hurriedly locked up the house. 'You call the vet from the car.'

As we left the village I managed to get through to Michelle on my mobile, and hurriedly filled her in, telling her we would be at the surgery with Monkey within twenty minutes.

'We'll be ready and waiting for him,' said Michelle grimly. 'But Julie – you know how serious this is. It may be too late.'

I blinked back tears as I hung up. Michelle was right – and she was just saying out loud what I knew was true, so I would be prepared if the worst happened. But the idea of something happening to my beloved Monkey was unthinkable.

'Hey,' said Glenn gently, briefly squeezing my arm, his eyes still fixed on the road ahead. 'It'll be OK. And if it's not, we'll get through it together.'

I smiled weakly, feeling a rush of gratitude for his solid, reassuring presence. 'Thank you. I really hope you're right.'

'What's wrong with him, anyway?' asked Glenn, and I realised I hadn't explained what all this was about. He'd just trusted that it was serious and come with me.

'It's called bloat,' I said. 'The dog's stomach twists, and it can cut off the blood supply, so that's why we have to get Monkey to the vet's really fast. If he doesn't get surgery, he'll die.'

Glenn reached out his hand again, linking his fingers briefly with mine. 'Better make sure we get him to the vet's in time, then,' he said and floored the accelerator, the tyres of the Shogun squealing. Thanks to Glenn's impressive driving, we got to Lisa's in record time. I hammered on the door until she flung it open, her face pale and streaked with tears. I pulled her in for a brief hug. 'You've done everything right,' I soothed her. 'We're here now – it's going to be OK.'

It was an empty promise – I knew the odds were very much not in our favour. But they were words Lisa needed to hear, and there was no time to dwell on whether it was right or wrong to give her false hope. Monkey desperately needed our help.

Chapter Twenty-Eight

The Waiting Game

'He's through here,' said Lisa, her voice trembling. She led us down the narrow hallway to the kitchen. The sight that greeted us caused me to stop dead in my tracks.

Monkey was laid out on his side on the cream tiled floor, and he was in a pitiful state. He was almost unrecognisable as the energetic, happy-go-lucky mutt I knew and loved. His belly was swollen and hard, and he was panting heavily. There was a disorientated, fearful look in his eye, and every so often he would retch hard, but no vomit came out. To see such a strong and vivacious animal look so weak and helpless was shocking.

Lisa had been right – this was a textbook case of bloat, and I was proud of her for recognising it so quickly. Her sharp observation could be what made the difference between whether Monkey lived or died.

'He's got so much worse in the last five minutes or so,' said Lisa, twisting her hands together anxiously. 'I would have taken him to the vet's straight away, but I can't lift him.'

Now weighing nearly eighty kilograms, Monkey was far too heavy for petite Lisa to hoist into the car alone, especially in this condition. With bloat you must keep the dog as still as possible, to prevent the stomach twisting further. There were three of us now, but we still had to proceed with extreme caution.

Lisa fetched the fleecy tartan blanket from his

bed and gently wriggled it under Monkey's prone form, Glenn and I carefully moving and rolling his body limb by limb to help her. Then Glenn and I each took an end of the blanket and, with Lisa supporting Monkey's body in the middle, we lifted him up in the makeshift sling. Staggering slightly under his weight, we inelegantly made our way outside, Lisa whispering words of reassurance to Monkey the whole way. Gently, we placed him in the back of my car. Monkey was brave and resolute, but the impact of being laid down caused him to give a heartbreaking whimper. Seeing him in so much pain made me feel sick, but I knew I had to hold it together for his sake.

'You're such a brave boy,' I told him. 'Hang on in there, we all love you so much.'

With that, we clunked the back door shut, and I refused to allow myself to consider the fact that this might be the last time we saw Monkey alive.

With Lisa on the back seat, her hand dangling into the boot so she could stroke Monkey's stricken form, we drove to the vet's in silence. I could tell Glenn was shocked by what he had seen, and he couldn't find any words to reassure us. Glancing in the rear-view mirror, I could see Lisa was crying again, tears rolling miserably down her cheeks. I couldn't think of anything to say that would make it better either, so I settled for a silent prayer instead. *Please, please let Monkey be OK.*

Glenn pulled into the parking space nearest the door of the surgery and the three of us resumed our awkward stretcher-bearing positions as we carried Monkey inside. As good as her word, Michelle was waiting for us, and she and one of the veterinary nurses rushed to help us carry him into her operating theatre, and lay him on the raised table. No sooner had we done so than the nurse was ushering us out, and without even a moment to say goodbye the door clicked shut – Monkey on one side, us on the other.

I heard a strangled cry of dismay, and realised

it had come from me. Of course, I knew there was no time to waste, but it had all happened so quickly. I knew Michelle and her team would do their absolute best for Monkey, but it hurt like hell not to be by his side to comfort him.

I sank into one of the plastic chairs that lined the waiting room, and put my head in my hands. Glenn and Lisa came to sit either side of me, and I could feel worry pulsing off them both, echoing my own.

'Julie?' began Lisa tentatively. 'Do you know what they'll be doing for Monkey now?' I looked up and saw the pleading expression on her face. She was desperate for any crumb that would reassure her.

'Well, I'm no vet, so we'll have to get the details from Michelle later,' I said, taking her hand in mine. 'But I guess they will be doing surgery to release the build-up of gas in his stomach. She'll probably use a tube or a stomach pump to do that, and that will save the tissue in his stomach and take the pressure off his organs. Hopefully she'll be able to untwist his stomach then.'

Lisa gulped. 'Sounds like a lot,' she said. 'Poor Monkey.'

'He's in safe hands now,' I said. 'And he'll be under anaesthetic, so he won't feel a thing. He'll already be much more comfortable now than he was ten minutes ago.'

Talking it through had been strangely calming, and I could feel my heartbeat slowing down to a more normal rate. Michelle had never let me down, and if anyone could save our precious dog, it was her.

Glenn cleared his throat. 'Listen, I don't know that dog even half as well as the two of you,' he said. 'But what I do know is that he's not the kind to give up without a fight. Didn't you say yourself, Julie, that no one should ever write him off?'

I smiled weakly. 'That's true,' I said. 'Although I think I was referring to situations where ham was on offer . . .'

'Even so,' chimed in Lisa, 'Glenn's right. Monkey has already overcome his fair share of obstacles – why should this be any different?'

We lapsed back into silence, but more comfortable this time. I could feel a flicker of hope building in my chest as the minutes ticked slowly by. Monkey would be OK, I told myself – he had to be, right?

Chapter Twenty-Nine

A Dreaded Disease

In the airless waiting room, time seemed to stretch and expand like a rubber band. The minutes inched by at a snail's pace, while all around us pet owners came and went, some happily wrangling puppies after routine injections, others looking anxious and pale as they led plodding dogs or carried out sickly cats in baskets. I could barely register anyone else, though: my thoughts were consumed by poor Monkey.

Bloat had been something that terrified me for

years, but fortunately no dog of mine had ever suffered it before. I had a friend whose Dobermann
had died of bloat, and ever since then I had felt
the prospect of it hanging like a spectre around
any work I did with big dogs.

Sadly, bloat is all too common in larger breeds
with deep chests. Great Danes, St Bernards,
Weimaraners, German shepherds and Labradors
are among those which are particularly suscepti-
ble. I wished breeders would make people more
aware of the risks, because often owners don't
realise something is wrong before it is too late.
The survival rate is not good, and if you don't act
fast, it's game over.

Working with big dog breeds, bloat was something my staff and I had to be constantly wary of.
They were all drilled on the symptoms, and I had
sheets detailing what to watch out for stuck up all
around our training HQ. It had felt like paranoia
at times, but now I was extremely grateful that I
had made awareness such a priority.

The causes of bloat are not fully understood, but one way to help prevent it is to avoid strenuous exercise after feeding. All my dogs always had a two-hour rest after their main meals, because I never wanted to take the risk. I knew for certain Lisa would have stuck by that rule, so exactly how Monkey fell victim was a mystery. Sometimes it can be caused by something as seemingly harmless as the dog drinking too much after eating, or jumping up at a funny angle. Ultimately, it was just terrible luck.

Just after six, when the surgery was shutting up, Michelle finally emerged through the plain white door at the end of the waiting room. Glenn, Lisa and I were immediately on our feet, searching her face for clues about Monkey's fate.

'It's good news,' said Michelle quickly, seeing how anxious we all were. 'For now.' The relief felt like a tidal wave that almost knocked me sideways, and I sank back into the chair again.

'He's pulled through the surgery and he's stable,'

Michelle went on. 'But we're not totally out of the woods yet. Come through and I'll explain.'

Glenn helped me back to my feet and, leaning heavily on him, I followed Michelle and Lisa into her examination room. Michelle spread her hands out on the table, which was covered with scratch marks from her many furry and feathered patients. Lisa, Glenn and I stood awkwardly on the other side, huddled against each other.

'I just want to start by saying thank you, for bringing him in so fast,' said Michelle. 'I don't know how things would have turned out if you had been even a couple of minutes later.' I squeezed Lisa's arm in gratitude. Her timely phone call had saved Monkey's life – something I would never forget.

'So, as you correctly identified, Monkey was suffering from gastric dilatation-volvulus,' Michelle continued. 'Bloat,' she translated, seeing our blank faces.

'His stomach had filled with air and the pressure was stopping blood from the hind legs and abdomen returning to his heart. That was causing his whole body to go into shock.'

It sounded even scarier and more painful hearing Michelle lay it out like that.

'First we had to treat the shock, bring his heart back to a normal level with intravenous fluids, and then we carried out the surgery to untwist his stomach,' Michelle explained. 'While I had him open I tacked his stomach to the abdominal wall – that's a procedure called gastropexy – which should stop it happening again.'

It was almost too much to take in, but this sounded positive. 'Thank you, Michelle,' I managed. 'So is he OK now?'

Michelle paused. 'The surgery was a success,' she said. 'That's the good news. But we will have to wait and see how he recovers. I would say the first five days are still very much touch and go.'

I took a sharp intake of breath, and Lisa put her

arm around me. 'I'm not saying that to scare you,' said Michelle gently. 'I just want you to be aware of how serious this is. About a third of dogs don't make it, and you have to be prepared for that. But so far, so good.'

Michelle explained that they would keep Monkey in overnight as he came round from the anaesthetic, monitoring his progress. If all was well, he'd be able to go home tomorrow – with strict instructions for rest and a very slow reintroduction of food for his delicate stomach.

'Don't worry, there will be someone with him the whole time tonight,' she reassured us. 'Julie, I'll ring you first thing tomorrow to update you on his progress, and then hopefully you'll be able to take him home to his own bed.'

We bid Michelle goodbye then trailed out to the car like shell-shocked survivors in a disaster movie. The carefree, sunny morning seemed for ever ago as we drove home in the gathering dusk, still preoccupied by the grave situation. Michelle's words kept ringing in my ears: 'The first five days are still very much touch and go.'

Worried that Lisa wouldn't want to be on her own, I asked her if she wanted to stay at ours, but she was determined to get back and make sure everything was ready for Monkey coming home the next day. Her fierce optimism gave me hope. If Lisa believed we'd be picking up Monkey in the morning, I should too.

After we'd dropped her at her door, Glenn drove us back to the cottage. Once inside, he wrapped me in his arms, and I let out the tension of the day in great shuddering sobs.

'Shh, it will be OK,' he soothed, kissing the top of my head. 'I'm here.'

My dogs were circling around our ankles, desperate to comfort me too. I always say that animals have a sixth sense for human emotion, and they know when you need them most. Glenn went to make us some tea and toast, and I collapsed on the sofa, snuggling up with Pickles on my lap, George and Ginelli either side, and Lala and Gypsy at my feet.

Monkey was in good hands, but as I looked at my dogs, so happy and settled by my side, I shuddered to think of him in the vet's, so far away from home. I knew he had a fighting spirit, but he was on his own. Not for the first time, I had to put my faith and trust in him, and hope he could beat this thing.

Chapter Thirty

Resting Times

Inevitably, I slept terribly, tossing and turning all night, haunted by nightmare visions of Monkey struggling to breathe.

By 5 a.m., I knew I wouldn't be getting back to sleep, so I got dressed and went downstairs to put the telly on to distract myself. It didn't work, exactly – I found I was just staring at the screen as the same news headlines were repeated on BBC News, then BBC Breakfast, not taking any of it in. At 7 a.m., the dogs were getting impatient for their usual morning walk, but I had to disappoint them.

'Sorry, baby,' I told Lala as she looked up at me imploringly, her paw on my knee. 'I've got to wait for an important phone call.'

Just before 8 a.m., the phone finally rang. I grabbed it on the first ring. 'Have you had a car accident that wasn't your fault?' intoned an automated message. I slammed the receiver down in fury. Just what I needed, a nuisance call.

'Hey, everything all right, Jules?' It was Glenn in his dressing gown and slippers, leaning on the living-room doorframe. He must have heard my shrieking as I hung up the phone.

'I just can't bear the waiting,' I told him, looking up at him with tired eyes. 'I hate not knowing how Monkey—'

I was interrupted by the phone buzzing again, and I hastily snatched it up.

'Hello?' I answered, my voice thick with anxiety.

'Hi Julie, it's Michelle. I'm pleased to tell you

Monkey is recovering well, and you can come and pick him up.'

And just like that, it felt like Christmas morning. I thanked Michelle profusely then, hands shaking, I dialled Lisa's number.

Like me, she picked up straight away, sounding just as scared and ill rested. I knew she'd be afraid I was ringing with the news she dreaded.

'It's fine, Lisa,' I reassured her immediately. 'He made it through the night – he can come home!'

Lisa gave a half-laugh, half-cry, but struggled to say much else. 'That's how I feel too,' I said. 'Meet you at the vet's in half an hour?'

Our relief was short lived, because as soon as Lisa and I got to the vet's Michelle was keen to impress on us how precarious Monkey's condition remained.

'He's had major surgery so it's going to be a long time before he is fully recovered,' she told us, her face serious. 'Your challenge is going to be to make sure he really rests – no playing, no exercise, nothing. He needs to stay as still as possible for the first few days.'

Michelle explained that we would have to introduce food little and often again, mindful of Monkey's delicate stomach. 'I'll want to see him in five days' time, and we can assess our next steps then,' she said. 'But if at any point he looks like he is taking a turn for the worse, call me straight away.'

Lisa and I nodded, taking it all in. Michelle's face softened. 'Listen, if anyone can get him back to health, it's you guys,' she said. 'It's hard work, but it's nothing you've not done before.'

'Thanks, Michelle,' I smiled. 'Can we see him now?'

'I'll just go and get him.' She disappeared through the door that led to the kennels where the vets kept their animal patients overnight, while Lisa and I stepped out into the waiting room.

'Do you still want me to have him?' Lisa

asked tentatively. 'Obviously I want to, but I'd understand if you'd rather take him home your-self. Like, you're way more experienced than me . . .' Her voice trailed off, and she looked at her shoes.

I couldn't lie, the thought had crossed my mind. Monkey's health was such a big responsibility and the control freak in me wanted to be the one by his side, making sure everything went to plan. But taking him back to the cottage would mean throwing him out of his routine and having to get him used to a new environment just at the time when he most needed familiarity. Then there were my boisterous dogs and cats to take into account: I couldn't guarantee they would give him the space and peace he needed to recover. And I trusted Lisa completely – if anyone would give Monkey the love and care I would have lav-ished on him if he was at mine, it was her.

'Hey, you can do this,' I said gently. 'He should be with you – it's what he would want. And I'll be with you every step of the way – you won't be on your own.'

Lisa smiled, then threw her arms around me. I laughed, and hugged her back. Her voice muffled as she spoke into my shoulder, she said, 'Thank you so much. I won't let you down.'

The sound of claws clickety-clacking on the laminate floor made us break apart abruptly. Spinning round, I saw Michelle leading Monkey towards us. He was moving slowly and gingerly, his bowed head encircled with a plastic cone to stop him licking his stitches. When he caught sight of us, I saw a flicker of affection pass across his face and he sniffed the air eagerly.

Lisa and I approached him slowly, not wanting to provoke him into trying to jump up in greeting. I spotted the wound on his stomach, red and stark, and where Michelle had shaved away his fur ahead of surgery. He was like a wounded soldier, and I felt my heart ache for him. You wouldn't want any dog to go through what he had, but Monkey was such a little treasure, he really didn't deserve it.

Monkey was delighted to see us, leaning against our legs, his tail wagging weakly as we kissed and stroked him. His body may be weak, but his soul was as affectionate and sweet as always.

Michelle accompanied us to the car park to help us hoist Monkey into the back of Lisa's car. 'Good luck,' she said, giving us both a hug. 'Remember – anything that concerns you, just call me.'

I followed Lisa's car back to hers, and together we gently carried Monkey into the house. Lisa had made up his bed in the living room with fleecy blankets and squashy cushions, and Monkey sighed as he gratefully sank into it. Awkward with the cone, it took him a moment to get comfortable, but as soon as he was he immediately fell asleep.

'He's exhausted, bless him,' I said. 'Maybe it won't be so hard ensuring he stays nice and still if he just wants to sleep all the time.'

Lisa was busying herself making tea, and now she handed me a stripy mug. 'I won't leave his side,' she told me fiercely. 'I promise.'

Over the next five days, Lisa was as good as her word. She watched Monkey like a hawk, even sleeping on the sofa so he wasn't on his own at night. I rang her first thing in the morning and last thing at night, and popped over twice a day to see how they were both getting on.

It was a scary time, but every time I saw Monkey I noticed an improvement. His eyes were getting brighter, his tail wagging more energetically, his bowl licked clean with greater enthusiasm. He still slept a lot, but as the days went on he started trying to move around a bit more. Lisa made sure he didn't bounce about too much, but it was nice to see him sniffing around her garden, enjoying the sun on his back.

Michelle was delighted with his progress and drew up a plan for increasing his food intake. She gave us the green light to start taking Monkey out for short walks – 'But keep him on the lead and no more than ten minutes at first, please,' she added.

It looked like Monkey was going to make it – and I couldn't have been happier. All I had wanted and prayed for was for him to be well. But what was less certain was whether he would ever work again. Would he get his full strength back? And if so, would he do so before *Harry Potter 5* started shooting in just four months' time?

I would need a Fang, and the idea of starting from scratch again, with a third dog, was both exhausting and upsetting. To me, Monkey was irreplaceable. I'd never find another Neapolitan mastiff quite like him. But his health had to come first.

So one afternoon I dug out the number for Debbie, at Mastiff Rescue UK. Maybe it was time to start searching again.

Chapter Thirty-One

Director's Mutt

I knew that I didn't have time to waste, but still there was something that stopped me calling Debbie. Time and again I would stare at the number, the phone in my hand, before putting down the receiver without dialling. What was holding me back?

If I was honest with myself, the idea of scouting for another Neapolitan mastiff seemed disloyal to Monkey. Silly really, as finding another dog wouldn't have ruled out using Monkey in the film, but to even start looking felt like I had given up on his fighting spirit.

When *Harry Potter and the Goblet of Fire* came out, I was disappointed to see Monkey's scenes didn't make the final cut, but that's just the reality of film-making, which I was used to by now. One of the reasons I really wanted him to work on the next film was so that he could secure his place in *Potter* legend.

What's more, Monkey was giving me less and less reason to doubt him. Once his stitches came out and he got to ditch the cone, he was much more like his old self. As autumn turned to winter, I often joined Lisa when she was taking him out for short walks on the lead, both of us bundled up in coats and scarves. In front of my eyes I could see Monkey's strength flooding back, as well as his natural curiosity and mischievous nature. As Michelle had predicted, with Monkey feeling better the hardest thing was making sure he didn't do too much. As usual he wanted to jump about and play, and couldn't understand why we didn't let him.

Just before Christmas, the script for *Harry Potter and the Order of the Phoenix* arrived. At the studios, I met up with the rest of the animal department so we could go through it together. This was part of our normal process – we would make notes on what animals we would need and brainstorm ideas for how we would train them and what they could bring to the shot to make it as effective as possible.

One of the most fun elements of this script was the call for about forty kittens, who would be filmed with numerous props and in little outfits to create the moving portraits that would appear on kitsch plates adorning the walls of Professor Umbridge's office. From the delighted squeals of the other trainers I knew there would be – excuse the pun – a cat fight over who worked on that particular project.

Scanning through, I noted that there were

several scenes that called for Fang, and that most of the moves were ones Monkey already knew. There were six weeks to go until filming started, and Monkey would just need refresher training. His fitness was really improving, and training would be a great way of letting him do more interesting things without being too active. It made up my mind: I was going to put my faith in him, no back-up required.

A few days later, I had a meeting with the new director, David Yates, to discuss our ideas and finalise training plans. When David was announced as the man in charge, it had raised a few eyebrows. He had only directed one film before and had mainly worked on award-winning TV – like political drama *State of Play* and *Sex Traffic*, a gritty tale of trafficked women. The storyline for the fifth film was darker and more political than ever before, and the producers wanted someone with David's eye to bring it to life in a powerful yet entertaining way. If producer

David Heyman thought he was the best man for the job, that was more than good enough for me.

When I met David at his office in Leavesden, I liked him immediately. He was quieter and more reserved than some of the directors I've worked with, but there was something about his softly spoken manner that put me at ease.

'I'm excited about seeing your animals in action,' he told me as the meeting drew to a close. 'Are there any returning from past films?'

'Yes, several,' I replied. 'Actually, there's one in particular ... the dog who plays Fang. Monkey. He's been in the wars since the last film but he's going to be fighting fit, and I think you'll love him.'

'I'm sure I will,' beamed David.

So that was it. I'd committed Monkey to the project, and as soon as the words were out of my mouth I knew he would be up to the task. The meeting over, I drove straight round to Lisa's house to tell her what I had decided.

'Oh, he'll definitely be up to it,' she told me, elated. 'Look at him now – he's got so much energy again, I know he'll be raring to get back to work.'

We laughed as Monkey chased his tail, almost toppling over. Trying to right himself, he staggered dizzily into Lisa's Christmas tree, sending ornaments scattering all over the floor.

Lisa sighed. 'That happens at least three times a day,' she said. 'I must be the only person who's decorated their tree not once but eighty-five times.'

Giggling, I helped her put the baubles back, hooking them on higher branches, 'although he's so big it makes no difference really,' according to Lisa.

I stayed for a mince pie, Monkey shoving his big, handsome head in my lap on the sofa and demanding I fuss him. We agreed Monkey would have a chilled Christmas at home, but come January, it was back to work. Looking down at those gorgeous puppy-dog eyes and that soppy expression, I realised how much I'd missed training with him. I couldn't wait to get started again.

Chapter Thirty-Two

Good Lassie

Christmas is one of the few times of the year I get a proper break, with most film productions winding down. It's all relative, of course; I still had all the animals to care for, so the usual early starts. But the festive period did give me the time to finally go to the cinema and see *Lassie*, a movie Monkey had shot just before he got ill.

It was a project I had been really excited to get involved with. As a child, *Lassie* was my favourite TV show, and watching the amazing work of the on-screen dogs was one of the things that inspired me to work with animals. So I was delighted when I heard about this movie, a remake of the 1945 original, and the eleventh film about the famously intelligent pooch with an extraordinary homing instinct.

Lassie is one of the most famous canine characters in film history – and alongside German shepherds Rin Tin Tin and Strongheart, who starred in silent movies, is one of only three dogs to be honoured on the Hollywood Walk of Fame.

The cast for the remake was a who's who of British acting talent, with Peter O'Toole, Samantha Morton, Edward Fox, Nicholas Lyndhurst and Steve Pemberton, among others. Of course, the real stars of the show were the rough collies who played Lassie. Because the character had so much screen time, three dogs were needed for the part; and all, ironically, were male: Carter, Mason and Dakota. They were incredibly beautiful animals, with long auburn-and-white coats and intelligent, foxy faces. If I'm honest, I was more excited about meeting these stunning creatures than any of the famous actors!

Our sister company in the States, Birds & Animals Unlimited, was to take the lead on the project as the three Lassies were all American dogs. The British version of the breed is smaller and doesn't have Lassie's trademark white blaze on the face, so wouldn't have been right for the film. Rough collies are also rarer over here, whereas the enduring legacy of Lassie means they are still a popular breed in the States.

The American team brought their squad of three dogs over from Los Angeles for the shoot in the luscious countryside of Ireland and the Isle of Man.

Meanwhile, Birds & Animals UK helped with a vast supporting cast of canine characters, including a guard dog owned by Peter O'Toole's character, the Duke of Rudling. As soon as I read through the scenes, I knew Monkey would be perfect for the part.

That's how he came to travel to Ireland with me, catching the ferry from Holyhead, to take up the role of Bosun. As usual, Monkey was delighted to be on a new adventure, and I was over the moon to have him all to myself for a few weeks. His part required him to do all the things he was good at – barking, growling and lying by the fire – and he pulled it off perfectly.

I have rarely been on a more dog-friendly set – which I guess is to be expected when the whole movie revolved around the animals. The director, Charles Sturridge, was happy for us to turn every scene into a game for the dogs involved, so they all thrived on doing their work.

My American colleagues had done a brilliant job with the Lassies. The two brothers, Carter and Dakota, were meant to be the stars, with Mason as understudy, but it soon became clear that Mason had a special quality that meant he should be the lead. He did most of the tricks, while the others were used as stunt doubles for certain scenes or when he was tired. I loved watching Mason work: he was another dog who just adored training and delivered everything with sparkling energy.

The film had a tight schedule – just three months – and it flew by. Monkey loved the fact that he had so many playmates, as did all the other animals, and there were plenty of high jinks between the filming sessions. It was fun for us trainers too: with so many of us working on the film, it was a great chance to bounce ideas off one another and pick up new techniques.

As animal trainers, we were used to fitting around the work of others, but on this film the tables were turned. Obviously, that took a bit of adjusting for the human actors. Peter O'Toole decided he was going to join in the general chaos, clearing his throat before each take by barking at top volume. The first time he did it, Monkey went mad and the two got drawn into a rather surreal 'bark off' – in which Monkey had the tactical advantage of actually being a dog!

Watching the film back in a quiet cinema one Tuesday lunchtime before Christmas, all these memories came flooding back. Monkey had relished being on the film set, playing with the other dogs and getting lots of attention from the cast and crew.

One of the final scenes had Monkey seeing off the baddie of the film – cruel servant Hynes, played by Steve Pemberton, who the audience had earlier seen beat Lassie. Monkey looked quite fearsome as he snarled and barked, before chasing Hynes out of the manor house. It was a proper performance – in real life, Monkey would have been more likely to lick Hynes's hand and demand a belly rub.

I was so proud of his work on *Lassie*, but I couldn't forget that it had been just weeks after the film wrapped that Monkey had been struck down with bloat. Knowing that he had come through that ordeal really was the best Christmas present I could possibly have had.

The rest of the festive season passed in a blur. We enjoyed spending time with our families, but it was also lovely returning to the cottage, shutting the door and digging into the Quality Street, with the dogs and cats curled up under the twinkling Christmas lights.

On Boxing Day, it's my tradition to take the dogs for a lovely walk, usually meeting Jo as well. This year it wouldn't feel right without Lisa and Monkey, so I invited them along too. Jo suggested Woburn Woods – 'It's perfect for Boxing Day – you'll see,' she told me mysteriously.

We met the girls in the car park, all of us dressed in new festive hats and scarves, and, in Glenn's case, a rather loud Christmas jumper.

'Merry Christmas!!!' cried Jo, flinging her arms

around us all. Her four dogs were going mad to see my five, and Monkey was predictably totally hyper, torn between wanting to play with Lala and Ginelli and demanding lots of attention from the human members of the party.

We headed into the redwood trees, squirrels scampering from the pathway, eagerly chatting about our various Christmases. 'I'm already looking forward to my turkey sandwich for lunch,' joked Lisa.

'Oh God, I don't think I want to see turkey ever again!' groaned Jo.

The narrow path opened out into a wide sandy track, where other groups of walkers, surrounded by dogs and kids, were making their way. Then I spotted something that made me gasp.

'Is that ... a Christmas tree?'

One of the little pine trees at the edge of the path had been carefully decorated with pretty baubles and strings of beads. It was definitely an amateur job – the mismatched decorations were dotted at irregular intervals, and whoever had done it obviously couldn't reach the higher branches – but the effect was still magical. We were right in the middle of nowhere – who had come all the way out here to decorate a living pine tree?

'That's right,' grinned Jo. 'No one knows how it started, but it's a bit of a tradition in these woods. People come out here and decorate their "wild" Christmas trees. There'll be a few more, you'll see.'

There certainly were, and we couldn't help competing with each other to see who could spot the most. Monkey seemed to understand the game, and whenever a Christmas tree came into view he'd race over to it and stand guard, panting happily.

'Is it just me, or is that daft dog actually a genius?' I asked Lisa.

She chuckled. 'I've always said he tries to read your mind, Julie,' she said. 'He's just a teacher's pet!'

I looked back at Monkey fondly. He was now trying to help Pickles with an enormous stick – him at one end and her at the other, totally mismatched in height. It was crazy to think how close he had come to not seeing this Christmas.

Now I needed him to return to *Harry Potter* and be a star again. Would his brush with death and the long recovery have taken their toll on what he would be able to deliver? I refused to entertain the prospect, but I can't say that it wasn't lurking at the back of my mind as we wandered back to the car. I needed Monkey to pull off another miracle.

Chapter Thirty-Three

The Steaks are High

January arrived soon enough, but I never dread going back to work. I guess it helps when you have your dream job, and get to play with animals all day.

On the first day we were scheduled to be back at Leavesden, I was already waiting eagerly by the front door of the cottage when Lisa drew up with Monkey. He bounced out of the car, beside himself to find he was back in his old routine. He was so full of beans he almost yanked Lisa's arm out as he dragged her up the path towards me. It was hard to believe this dog had been at death's door just a few months ago.

'Definitely hasn't got the back-to-work blues,' laughed Lisa. She handed his lead over to me and I loaded him into the car, then Lisa waved us off as we pulled away. 'Good luck, Monkey! Be good!'

Monkey didn't settle at all on the drive to the studios, sitting bolt upright and taking in the scenery whizzing past. Had he worked out where we were going? I think he must have done – and he couldn't wait to get there.

As we drew into the car park at the training ground, Monkey started whimpering with excitement. I couldn't help but laugh; it was wonderful to have an animal who just loved to work. 'You guessed it, Monkey,' I told him. 'We're back in your favourite place.'

And just like that, it was as if we'd never been away. We fell straight back into the usual training regime and Monkey took to it with ease. He had to do a lot of barking in this film, so we worked on that, his deep, booming 'WOOF' ringing out across the set.

In between training sessions, Monkey was up to his usual tricks, running in mad loops and trying to distract anyone he could with his crazy antics. Surgery hadn't dampened any of his energy; if anything, he had even more.

Luckily, he had a new playmate, in the form of Cleod, the Scottish deerhound I was training to play Padfoot, the dog Harry's godfather Sirius Black is able to transform himself into. Tall and rangy, with delightfully scruffy iron-grey fur, Cleod had been loaned from a lovely breeder based in the Peak District. He was a previous winner of Best Puppy at Crufts, but hadn't done any film work before.

While he was a super-sweet boy, Cleod wasn't the easiest to train. It wasn't his fault: deerhounds are very laid back in nature and have a limited attention span, so it can take them a bit longer to pick things up. Cleod also didn't like shiny floors and was nervous around new people so we had a lot of work to do before he would be ready for his scenes, which would see him running down a train platform constructed in the studios.

I hoped that Monkey's buoyancy and fearless nature would rub off on him, so I was happy to let them play together between sessions. They soon became firm friends, and I'd often catch them dozing side by side – large and larger!

As the weeks went on, Monkey went from strength to strength. He really thrived in our training sessions, and the basics came back to him in no time.

With filming imminent, I needed to prepare him for his main scene. Not that this would be too much of a trial. If Monkey had written the script himself, it could not have been more perfect for him. He would be lying by the fire in Hagrid's hut, while Hagrid himself dabs at wounds he has sustained with a big slab of steak. Fang is watching him greedily, and starts barking – quietly at first, then getting louder and louder as he demands the meat. Hagrid gives in and tosses the big juicy steak to Fang, who chews it up hungrily.

What dog wouldn't enjoy filming a scene which requires them to gobble up a delicious chunk of premium meat? The problem was I couldn't practise endlessly with a full-sized steak – it wouldn't be good for Monkey's health, to say nothing of the cost. But I did need to prepare him, so the excitement of getting a slab of beef thrown to him wouldn't break his concentration.

During our practice sessions, a rubber toy stood in for the steak – which Monkey enjoyed thoroughly all the same. As filming drew closer, I started chucking some bits of chicken his way to chew up as we rehearsed, instead of as a treat afterwards, and he couldn't believe his luck. Despite this, he managed to keep his focus, and

I hoped he'd be able to do the same when we did it for real.

The scheduled day for the scene arrived with a 5 a.m. wake-up call, my alarm jolting me from the midst of sleep. I'd arranged to pick up Monkey from Lisa's rather than have her bring him to me as it was so early. When I arrived, Lisa was in her pyjamas and dressing gown, but Monkey was bright eyed and raring to go.

'It's almost as if he knows that he's going to get the best lunch of his life today!' I joked to Lisa as we loaded him into the car. She smiled sleepily.

At the studios, I gave Monkey his usual pre-filming groom, then we set off on foot for the main set, where Hagrid's hut had been constructed. I had several spare slobber towels in my bag – I definitely didn't want a repeat performance of Drool-gate!

As usual, there were lots of people bustling around, setting up the equipment. But Monkey could sense something was different. I caught him sniffing the air and staring with intent at a shaven-haired prop master, who had a large cool bag in his hands. Monkey could smell the steak.

As Robbie, Emma, Rupert and Daniel all arrived and took their positions on set, Monkey's tail wouldn't stop wagging. But instead of giving his co-stars their usual slobbery welcome, his eyes never left the prop guy, Jaber, who nervously held the bag closer to him.

Once everyone was positioned to David's liking, Jaber finally unzipped his bag. He took out an enormous juicy steak and handed it to Robbie. Monkey licked his lips, and I rushed in to quickly wipe away the drool that had started to form.

'Listen, Monkey, I know it's distracting but you've got to focus on me, OK?' I whispered to him as I gave him a final pat. He swivelled round to lock his eyes on me, and I knew he wasn't going to let me down.

'How many steaks do we have?' David asked.

'Er, we've got five,' confirmed Jaber.

'We don't have too many takes then, everyone,' David said to the room, and I saw his eyes flick over to me. 'So let's get this right.'

There was silence as a few final adjustments were made to the lighting, and then David called 'Action!'

Standing just behind the camera, I gave the signals to Monkey. I knew him so well that I could always tell what he was thinking, and today I could sense him fighting something inside that was telling him to leap up at Robbie and grab the steak. I kept my commands low and calm, and I saw the good angel in Monkey defeat the naughty devil. On my cue, he started barking just as we'd practised.

'Go on, you have it then, you dozy dog,' said Robbie as Hagrid, and tossed the hunk of meat to Monkey, who fell upon it like he had never eaten before. I kept telling him to stay, so he wouldn't run off before the cameras had stopped rolling, and I could hear the chuckles of the cameramen as they zoomed in on Monkey having the time of his life.

When the call came for cut, I rushed in to take the rest of the steak off Monkey so he didn't make himself sick by gobbling it all at once. I trusted him completely, which was why I didn't have any fear as I removed it from his powerful jaws. He looked up at me mournfully as I confiscated it but didn't so much as growl – quite an achievement, as even the calmest of dogs can get defensive over food.

'Don't worry, boy, I think you're going to get to do it again,' I said, winking at him.

Sure enough, David wanted us to give it another go – 'Although that was almost perfect,' he reassured the cast.

This time, Monkey knew what to expect – and I don't think it was a coincidence that he barked with even more gusto than usual. His eyes widened as the second steak was tossed his way – he thought all his birthdays had come at once!

Two takes proved enough to get the scene in

the bag, but Monkey still managed to consume an impressive amount of meat; I made a mental note to remind Lisa to give him a smaller meal that evening. I was watching Daniel, Rupert and Emma making a fuss of him, when Jaber approached me.

'Don't let him know you've got another three steaks in there,' I smiled, gesturing at his cool bag.

Jaber laughed, then handed me a package of the leftovers of the meat we'd used during filming. 'Put it in his dinner – he deserves it,' he told me. 'It's thanks to him getting it in two that my partner and I will have steak tonight!'

I grinned, and took the spoils – cut up into chunks, this would be the perfect training aid. 'Thanks,' I said. 'And enjoy your steak – try to eat it a bit more calmly than Monkey!'

It was a memorable day, and probably Monkey's favourite on set so far. But there was something coming up which was going to prove even more special.

Chapter Thirty-Four

A Wish Come True

It was towards the end of filming *Harry Potter and the Order of the Phoenix* that the set got a very special visitor.

Her name was Molly, and she was nine years old. We had been prepared for her arrival several weeks earlier, in a meeting of the various heads of department. Molly was a VIP, and it was imperative that the day she spent with us was the most magical, fun and memorable that it could possibly be.

The *Harry Potter* producers didn't exactly make a habit of showing children around the set, which was big and complicated. But Molly was different – and for her, they were happily making an exception.

Why? Because Molly had an aggressive kind of leukaemia, something she had been battling since she was four years old. More than half of her life had been spent in and out of hospital, having chemotherapy that made her feel terribly sick and caused her beautiful chestnut curls to fall out.

The doctors and nurses who treated her became more familiar faces than her teachers and school friends, with Molly forced to miss swathes of the school year while she fought to stay alive.

Her childhood had been sadly interrupted – and she had more cares and worries than most adults. She needed a day when she could be a kid again, forget the gravity of her situation and have an injection of hope and excitement.

That's where the Make-A-Wish Foundation got

involved. The charity had visited Molly to see what she wanted to do more than anything else in the world. She was a huge *Harry Potter* fan, so she knew what her wish would be immediately: she wanted to visit the film set, and see how the magic was made.

I don't think I was the only member of the crew with tears in my eyes as Janice, a Wishgranter from the charity, related Molly's story in the meeting. She took us through a slideshow of pictures of Molly, including photos of her with tubes in her nose, others giving a thumbs-up from a hospital bed. It would be a privilege to give this brave little girl the experience of a lifetime.

When the meeting ended, I made for the door, but Janice called me back.

'It's Julie, right? The head animal trainer?'

'Yes, that's right,' I replied. 'Thanks so much for the presentation – we all can't wait to meet Molly.'

'That's great,' smiled Janice. 'I just wanted to give you a heads-up – Molly is also a really big animal lover, so I know visiting your department will be one of the highlights of her day. Anything you can do for her would be really appreciated.'

'Absolutely,' I nodded. 'She can handle the animals and have a go at training. We'll make it really special. What's her favourite animal, do you know?'

'Dogs,' said Janice. 'Especially big ones.' I smiled to myself – I knew just the guy for the job.

I was determined Molly's visit to our training HQ would be absolutely perfect. In the days leading up to her arrival, the team and I cleaned it from top to bottom. She was due to visit us just after lunch, having toured other parts of the set in the morning, so that gave us time to get the animals looking their best too. The cats were brushed, the feathers of the owls fluffed, and Monkey had another chaotic bath.

'Someone special is coming to see you today,

Monkey,' I told him, as I towelled him down afterwards. 'You have to be extra gentle with her, OK? But I think she's going to love you.'

Monkey nuzzled into my shoulder as if he understood what I was saying. I knew I didn't have anything to worry about as far as he was concerned – he always knew the right thing to do when kids were involved.

Molly, her parents, the people from the charity and their guides from the production staff were due with us at 2 p.m., but as I had expected, they were running a bit late. There was so much to see at the *Harry Potter* studios, and I knew they had probably been sidetracked by my passionate colleagues who would have been delighted to explain their work and let Molly in on some of the secrets.

I imagined that at the costume department they'd have dressed her up in wizarding robes, at the creature effects department let her get up close to animatronic models of phoenixes and hippogriffs, and at special effects amazed her with the computer-generated magic of the green screen. She was also due to meet some of the cast, who would be their usual charming selves. I hoped visiting the animal department after all that wouldn't prove to be an anticlimax!

Finally, we saw the golf buggies carrying the Make-A-Wish party coming down the track from to the main set. The other trainers and I hastily assembled to greet them, along with some of the most famous animals. Jo had ginger Persian Crackerjack, who played Crookshanks, in her arms. Guillaume had snowy owl Gizmo, better known as Hedwig, perched on his arm. And I had my beloved Monkey sitting at my side, his tongue lolling out in anticipation as he watched the convoy approach.

The golf buggies parked up, and I got my first glimpse of Molly. She was a tiny little thing, squeezed in between a young couple who must be her parents. She was wearing an oversized

Harry Potter T-shirt and flowery leggings, a pink patterned bandana covering her head. Her face was small and pale, but lit up by the biggest grin.

'Hello, welcome to the animal department!' I called, waving. 'How's your day been so far?'

The party piled out of the buggies, full of chatter about all the amazing things they had seen already and how lovely everyone had been. But I quickly clocked Molly wasn't participating in the conversation – because she was completely transfixed by Monkey.

Ever obedient, Monkey was still sitting by my side, but his gaze was on Molly. She was a little shy and hung back at first.

'It's OK, Molly, he's super friendly,' I reassured her. 'He's a big softie – loves a cuddle.'

Molly nodded, and drew closer. She reached out her small hand and laid it on Monkey's colossal head, stroking him gently.

'Hello, Fang,' she murmured.

'Oh, his real name is Monkey,' I told her. 'Suits

him much better – he's a lot more cheeky than he is scary, you see.'

Molly giggled, rubbing Monkey behind the ears. 'Good boy, Monkey.'

My heart swelled with pride as I watched Monkey with this brave little girl. He was so gentle, so soft in his movements, as if he knew this was not the time to be boisterous. He was looking at her with an expression of instant love, and by the look on Molly's face I could tell it was mutual.

'OK, we've got lots to show you here!' I said. 'And Monkey can come with us while we do the tour. You can hold his lead – what do you think?'

Molly beamed as I handed her Monkey's leash. He trotted patiently at Molly's side as I led her and her family around the training ground. Her proud parents happily snapped away as Molly posed with an owl perched on two clenched fists. I introduced her to Max, my tabby cat who played Mrs Norris, and she squealed with delight when

Max did his party trick of leaping up onto her shoulder. We visited the rats in their run and fed bacon scraps to the ravens in their aviary. Molly listened, rapt, as I told her what we did to train the animals for the film, absent-mindedly stroking Monkey's head the whole time.

I could tell she had made an immediate connection with my lovely dog, so I knew she'd relish the chance to train him. We went into one of the paddocks and I gave her some scraps of chicken. Monkey was instantly on high alert, his ears pricked forwards – he knew a treat was coming his way.

'OK, hold it in your hand like this,' I told Molly, showing her how to pinch the treat between her thumb and forefinger and hold it so Monkey could see. 'Now, we give the hand signal like this, and say "Mark!"'

'Mark!' Molly repeated, then clapped her hands as Monkey ran to a wooden block on the other side of the paddock.

'Now call him back . . .' I started, but Molly was ahead of me.

'Monkey, come!' He trotted over obediently and took the treat from Molly's outstretched hand as carefully and gently as if he was handling a baby bird.

I showed Molly some of Monkey's other tricks, and she adored the chance to give him the commands and reward him with the bits of chicken.

'You're a natural!' I said as Monkey rolled over for her.

'I'm going to be an animal trainer when I grow up,' she told me confidently. Out of the corner of my eye, I saw her mum wipe a tear away. From what Janice had told me, the doctors were by no means certain that Molly would live to adulthood. I hoped with all my heart that she would.

Finally, it was time to say goodbye. Molly posed for one last picture with her new canine pal, provoking gales of laughter as he inevitably got slobber on her clothes, then threw her arms around Monkey. He made a contented little noise as he snuffled into her neck.

'Bye bye, Monkey,' Molly told him. 'You're the best dog ever.'

I had a tear in my own eye as we waved them off, Molly badgering her parents about whether they could get a Neapolitan mastiff puppy. She was obviously a very poorly girl, but she still had a child's capacity for wonder and imagination. I hoped the happy memories of today would get her through the hard times to come.

I turned to Monkey and scratched him behind his ears, where he liked it best. 'She's not wrong,' I told him. 'You're pretty special: you know that, right?' Monkey just looked back at me, and I knew he wouldn't agree. He was just being himself – loving, trusting and kind – and he didn't think there was anything special about that.

Molly was the first of several Make-A-Wish children who visited us over the years, and each time was as poignant and inspiring as the last.

Monkey was always the star of the show, and no matter how shy the child, he could be relied upon to put them at ease.

I'm proud of everything that Monkey did, but those moments with those special children perhaps meant the most.

Whenever I think of him, so loving and gentle, I am always reminded how the smallest kindness – and a little bit of faith – can transform a life. He was one of a kind – my sweet, crazy, cheeky Monkey.

Epilogue

I don't like to dwell on how we lost Monkey – it feels wrong to focus on his death when he was always so full of life. After he survived his bloat emergency, it felt as if he was indestructible. His spirit was so irrepressible, his energy so boundless, that it was impossible to imagine a world without him.

In reality, we were blessed to have him for as long as we did. He was eleven when he passed away, which is remarkable for a Neapolitan mastiff, as they usually only live to eight or nine.

Monkey went on to work on the seventh

Harry Potter film, before a very happy retirement at Lisa's, which involved lots of walks at the reservoirs, endless love and attention and the odd photo opportunity as a former star of *Harry Potter*. I still saw him regularly, and he loved coming with me to the village show in Long Marston every year and posing with lots of eager children.

When the end came, it was mercifully fast. Lisa noticed one day that he was struggling to swallow, and we ran him down to the vet's. The diagnosis didn't take long – Monkey had a very aggressive tumour in his throat, and it was impossible to operate.

Everyone who knew him was devastated by the news – especially Lisa and me. It was terrible, feeling so helpless. Often, when an animal gets cancer, surgery is possible and you have a choice about what to do. But we couldn't do anything to help our sweet baby boy.

Lisa took him home and I was over there every

day, trying to squeeze every last cuddle out of Monkey's limited time left with us. We liquidised all his favourite foods so he could manage meals more easily, but after less than two weeks it had got to a point where even the softest of dinners was too hard for him to swallow.

Monkey was getting weaker and weaker, and it was like a sucker punch every time I arrived at Lisa's house to find him subdued and sad. He would still wag his tail when he caught sight of one of us, and wriggle with happiness if we crouched by him to stroke his handsome head. But he was fading, and we knew what we had to do.

Together, Lisa and I made one final pilgrimage to the vet's. I've had to do this with hundreds of animals over the years, but it never gets any easier. The price we pay for the love of an animal is the pain of saying goodbye – and it is a hefty price.

Sometimes I find it just too difficult to be there at the moment one of my animals is put to sleep, but I knew I had to be by Monkey's side. Over the years he had worked so hard for me, brought joy to so many others and loved the people in his life so fiercely. Stroking his paw as he left this world was the least I could do.

Lisa was in floods of tears as the injection went in, but I tried to bite mine back as I felt his warmth ebbing away.

'The world wrote you off, but you never stopped fighting,' I told him. 'You taught me faith and trust will never go unrewarded, and I will always love you for that. Goodbye, my bonkers Monkey man.'

And with that, he was gone. I sobbed all the way home and for most of the following week. I just couldn't get my head around the fact that I would never see that crazy, soppy, madcap dog again. But then I got a call that would change my perspective.

It was Gordon, my old friend from the *Harry Potter* prop department. I hadn't spoken to him in ages, so I was surprised to see his number flash up on my phone.

'Hi Jules,' he said. 'I heard on the grapevine about Monkey and I wanted to say how sorry I was to hear the news. He was a wonderful dog.'

I gulped back the emotion I could feel rising in my throat. 'Thanks, Gordon, that's lovely of you to say,' I said, my voice faltering.

'So, the real reason I'm calling is to ask, have you been to the Warner Bros Studio Tour yet?'

I paused, confused. The Studio Tour was an attraction that had opened at Leavesden in 2012, offering a glimpse inside the making of the *Harry Potter* films.

Although it had been open over a year, I hadn't been; having been involved in the making of the films for over ten years, it didn't seem like I would have too much to learn. Why Gordon was ringing me up to ask if I had gone was completely beyond me.

'Er, no, I haven't,' I said. 'Should I?'

'I know it seems like a weird thing to say, but I really think you should,' said Gordon. 'I don't want to ruin it, but there's something I think you'll be really pleased to see.'

I tried to press him further, but Gordon remained tight-lipped. We changed the subject and chatted some more before saying goodbye. I hung up the phone, still mystified.

Gordon wasn't the kind of person to wind me up – especially when he knew I was grieving for Monkey. On a whim, I pulled my laptop towards me, googled the attraction, and booked a ticket for the following day.

I arrived just after eleven the next morning, and joined the throngs of *Potter* fans jostling to get into the Great Hall, the first set on the tour. Along with many of the other iconic settings, the Hall had been dismantled piece by piece and rebuilt here for visitors.

It felt surreal, wandering through the sets that had been so familiar to me for so many years.

I took in the props and costumes, the screens showing clips from the movies and the boards of trivia, but I still couldn't work out why Gordon had been so keen for me to come.

Then I rounded a corner, and saw it. There was Hagrid's hut, recreated in precise detail. And on the wall beside it, a projection – of Monkey in action.

I drew closer, my mouth falling open in wonder. It was a short clip of me putting Monkey through his paces, explaining how I taught him to do various tricks. I couldn't even remember the day it was shot – the crew were always filming little behind-the-scenes vignettes because they knew the interest in how the movies were made would be intense.

I was transfixed to see Monkey alive again, in front of my very eyes. In the clip he was watching me with utter devotion, responding seamlessly to my commands as I guided him through the training drills. There was a bit where he almost stumbled – typical Monkey clumsiness – and at the end he jumped up for a treat, his whole body wagging with happiness, not just his tail. His personality shone through the screen: it couldn't have encapsulated him more perfectly.

I don't know how long I stood and watched the clip on a loop, my eyes filling with tears. For the first time since I had said goodbye to Monkey, I realised he wasn't really dead. He would live on, for *Potter* fans and for everyone who remembered him.

Forget the rest of the wizarding world – for me, this right here was the real magic.

How to Know if a Breed is Right for You

I believe that one of the reasons Monkey's original owners abandoned him was because they hadn't done their research on his breed. Once he stopped being a cute puppy and turned into a big and demanding dog, they didn't want him any more. Sadly, this happens far too much. People rush into buying a cute puppy with no idea what caring for an adult dog will entail. Rescue centres are full of dogs who have been abandoned when they are one or two years old, because the owners decided they couldn't cope. If only they had properly considered their lifestyle and what sort of dog would be compatible, this sad fate could have been avoided.

Here's my guide to what things you need to consider when choosing a breed that is right for you, your family and your lifestyle.

Do your research

Read up
The internet has a wealth of information about different breeds, but don't get distracted by the cute pictures. The Kennel Club's Breed Information Centre is a good place to start.

Meet in person
The annual Discover Dogs show and Crufts are great places to meet lots of different breeds and their owners.

Talk to an owner

If you have friends or family members who have the breed you're interested in, ask them lots of questions – and make sure they tell you the bad as well as the good. If you can, borrow their dog for a weekend and see how you get on.

Contact a breed club

Every breed has at least one dedicated organisation. Get in touch for information on personality, health and how to find a breeder.

Puppy or rescue?

If you do decide to get a puppy, make sure you find a responsible breeder.

But I would always recommend adopting a rescue if you can. They have so much love to give, and in the right home can be the most rewarding animals.

If you are after a particular breed, many breed

clubs run a rescue service – like the one that helped me find Monkey. It is even possible to find a rescue puppy.

Which dog is right for you?

How much exercise will you be able to provide your dog?

All dogs need daily exercise, but some breeds require much more than others, so make sure you can provide it. A dog not getting enough exercise can be naughty and destructive.

Do you or anyone in your household have allergies?

Some breeds don't shed their coat so are better for allergy sufferers. But no dog is 100 per cent hypoallergenic, so be prepared to groom regularly and wash the dog bed often.

How much time can you spend on grooming?

Dogs with longer coats will need lots of brushing as well as regular trips to the groomer. Some breeds also have a strong smell, or drool a lot, like Monkey, so make sure you consider this too.

How much space do you have?

If you live in a flat or don't have much of a garden, a smaller breed might be better. If you have the space for a big dog, you should also consider whether you will be able to physically handle a dog that might be heavier and stronger than you. And think about whether its size will make it difficult to find someone to look after your dog when you are away.

What's your experience of dogs?

Some breeds are easier to train than others, and if you are a first-time owner you may want to get one that's not too tricky. Breed clubs will be able to advise.

What's a typical temperament for the breed?

Of course, there are always exceptions to the rule, but most breeds were developed for specific working or aesthetic purposes. That can mean that they tend to have certain personality traits. Some breeds might be less friendly with strangers, or more inclined to bark, or dig. Make sure you find a dog whose personality you can handle.

Do you have children under ten, or other pets?

Some breeds are more suited to spending time with children and animals than others. This is vital to consider.

Once you've chosen your breed, you still need to find the perfect dog. If you are buying a puppy, make sure you see it with its mother and siblings, and how it interacts. Make sure the breeder is Kennel Club Assured and follows breeding guidelines.

Julie Tottman has been rescuing and training animals for the movies for over twenty-five years. Her credits include *Game of Thrones*, *Harry Potter* and *101 Dalmatians* among hundreds of others. She is a major advocate for animal welfare and feels very lucky to have her dream job.

The first book in the
Paws of Fame series

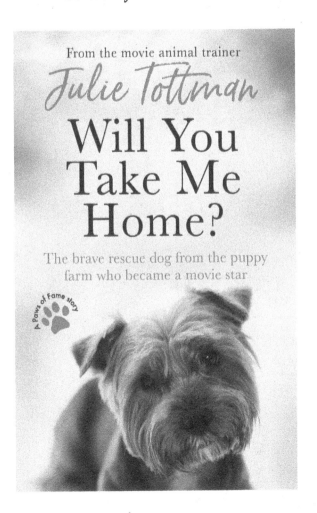

From the movie animal trainer

Julie Tottman

Will You
Take Me
Home?

The brave rescue dog from the puppy
farm who became a movie star

A Paws of Fame story